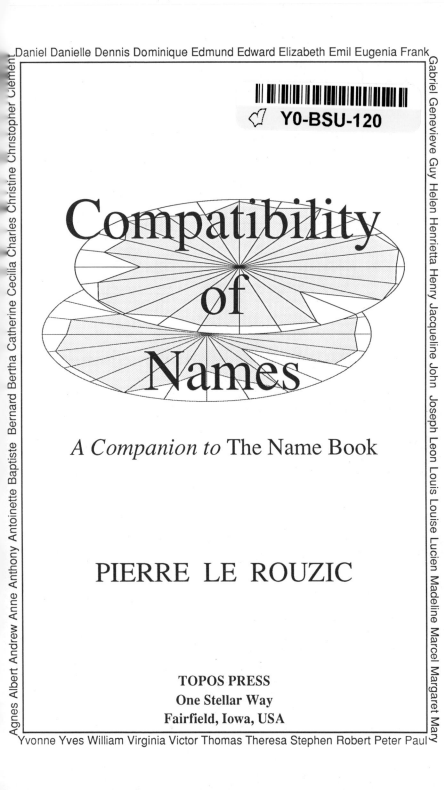

Y0-BSU-120

Compatibility of Names

A Companion to The Name Book

PIERRE LE ROUZIC

TOPOS PRESS
One Stellar Way
Fairfield, Iowa, USA

COMPATIBILITY OF NAMES

Printed in the United States of America.
92   91   90   89   3   2   1

ISBN 0–9622069–1–1

CONTENTS

PART I:

PART II:

PART III:

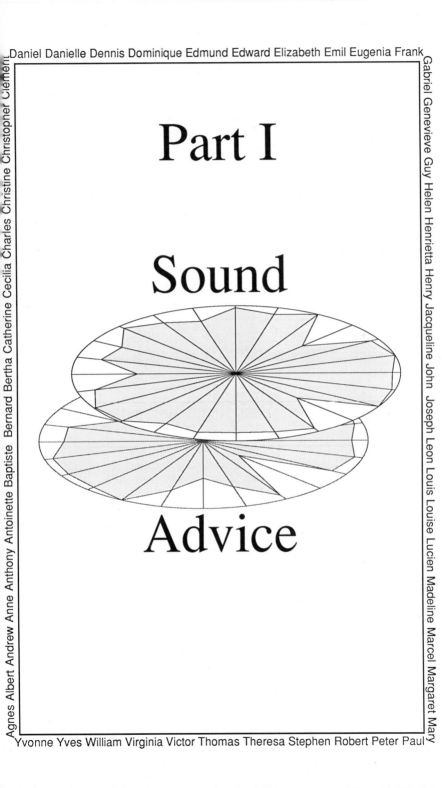

Part I

Sound

Advice

SOUND ADVICE

Who among us has not said at some point, "Oh, that Olga, I can't stand the sight of her!" or "James is the epitome of perfection!"

If one is honest with oneself and takes a moment to reflect a little, one would quickly see that we can't put our finger on anything definite that we object to in poor Olga, and that James has always been beyond reproach in our eyes.

At other times, we might be surprised to find that a particular person doesn't seem to notice the attention we lavish on them, our advances towards them, and remains completely indifferent to our presence. Conversely, the overly eager behavior of some man or woman around us might bother us deeply, when we feel we should have a more amicable, even sentimental, attitude towards them. Here again, the obstruction has no apparent basis in reality, and we will be mistaken if we try to reflect on it to locate its cause. Furthermore, no amount of reasoning with ourselves will be able to overcome the suspicion, even aversion, that we feel. It would seem in such cases that our polarity repels that of the other person like a magnet, even—or especially—when our partner is most attracted to us.

From where comes this lack of understanding, even opposition? In order to explain it, one might come up with a thousand sophisticated hypotheses, which somehow don't seem completely convincing: a kind of physique we don't like, a means of expression that displeases us, a possessiveness that disturbs us, or whatever... Why not appeal to the ancient Romans, who were fond of saying: "*Seguax, fuguax. Fuguax, seguax,*" or "Follow me, and I will run from you. Run from me, and I will follow you"?

Beyond all this literature, an explanation exists whose profound truth may never have occurred to us, namely the magnetic aura created around a person by the repetition of the sound of their name.

THE RESONANCE OF NAMES

Every name possesses, in an absoloute sense, a vibration that is distinctly its own. I have discussed this topic in *The Name Book*. This sound is, in some fashion, the signal of the man or woman who bears it. It is like a jingle, repeated thousands of times, which evokes a particular resonant universe.

Yes, a name is certainly the signal of an individual, their secret melody, a means of identification that is immediate and replete with affective associations. But how to take stock of this phenomenon? Why is it that the messages emitted by some names reach me distinctly, while others only reach me in a way that is jumbled, deformed, inaudible, and annoying? Is it that their transmitter is deficient (the most egotistical explanation) or that my receiver is not sensitive enough (the most heroic explanation)?

The whole problem of relationships arises in this way, for one will quickly realize that there exist, as in haemotology, universal transmitters, which everyone receives, and receivers that can pick up signals from all over the world, visible and invisible. This is the explanation for how someone could be a genius on the one hand or a saint on the other! And then, there is a whole host of specific sub-groups that transmit on wavelengths that few can receive, or those which can only receive a very restricted band of wavelengths.

In this light, we can imagine that it should be possible to evaluate how well a person with a particular name, endowed with specific vibrational qualities, can relate to another name with characteristics that are similar, analogous, or compatible. Thus we have arrived at the heart of the sentimental, family, and business life of the men and women of our world. How exciting!

EVERYTHING BECOMES COMPLICATED!

It takes courage to state that in place of the simple concept of equal and reciprocal relationships, we should subsitute the much more elaborate concept of personalized response.

Let me clarify this with an example. If I tell you that Frank relates to Patricia 80%, it would be natural to assume that, in return, Patricia relates to Frank 80% as well. But that is not the case. Here is where the situation becomes complicated. Patricia only relates to Frank 50%!

Let me explain. It wouldn't occur to anyone to stroke a cat's fur in the wrong direction, for fear of all kinds of feline drama one might imagine or scars that one might incur. Well, this is the suicidal maneuver we give into throughout the length of our lives. A successful man is he who follows the simple principle of not going against the current. It is good to know what is good sense, and it is here that humanity seems most lacking in discrimination.

In the world of affectivity, marriage, education of children, business, etc., it is very necessary to know which way the "fur" of the other person lies. This may appear to be anecdotal, but everything depends on the way in which we approach someone. On this matter, there are many animal trainers and tamers who can give us excellent advice!

And so we arrive at the problem of compatibility, which is to say the understanding or misunderstanding that can arise between two people whose names are harmonious or disharmonious with each other. Here is a clear explanation: a Bernard relates to a Peter 30%, which is not very much. From this one could deduce that whenever a Peter has some business with a Bernard, he should proceed prudently and avoid any direct confrontations, because Bernards are habitually mistrustful of Peters. On the other hand, Peter relates to Bernard 65%, which shows that if a Bernard makes an effort to control himself and tries to make himself understood, he will find in Peter a listener who is more attentive, if not easier to convince. In the following pages, you will have occasion to notice that considerable differences exist between the way that A relates to B and B relates to A.

You can easily imagine how interesting it is to determine the type of communication that might exist between you and a partner, whoever they may be! Knowing your personality equation with a man or woman whom you have to deal with doesn't necessarily simplify things, but it serves to put you on guard against precipitous conclusions, compromising carelessness, or hasty propositions.

A "VADE-MECUM"

It would make me happy if the work that you have in hand could be for you what the Latins called a *vade-mecum*, or, come (*vade*) with (*cum*) me (*me*). I actually feel that this little manual deserves to be kept on your person to be consulted on many occasions throughout life.

My name is Peter and I meet a Dominique, a charming young lady who makes a deep impression on me at a party. I consult my *vade-mecum* and find that I can relate to her 95%. Controlling my enthusiasm, I look up the degree to which this Dominique can relate to a Peter and I discover to my great joy the same percentage of 95%. Bravo, but don't get carried away! I am forewarned—all is winnable, but not yet won. How many certain victories have thus been confounded, torpedoed by the certainty of success!

Imagine that I am called Mary and that I present myself before a personnel manager whose name is Vince. While waiting for him to receive me, I consult my booklet and I discover, to my terror, that the percentage of my ability to relate to this formidable man is only 20%! This only adds to my anguish. On the other hand, I find that Vince relates to Mary 60%. Not a huge percentage, but better than nothing and this gives me reason to hope.

And so, with the knowledge of these compatibilities, I construct in my little head a battle plan based on two elementary arguments: first, that under no circumstance must I display the least coolness towards this man who, nevertheless, will chill me when I approach; second, it is important, on the contrary, that I increase the moderate interest that he has in me spontaneously with a dynamic and constructive attitude. And since I never leave home without *The Name Book*, I glance quickly at the personality portrait for Vincent and enter the office like a gladiator entering the arena, armed with certainty and confident of my fate.

NOT TO THROW THE HELVE AFTER THE HATCHET

You are married, and you consult your *Compatibility of Names* booklet... You, Michael, are stupefied to find that you only relate 50% to the Aurelia you married 15 years ago, while Aurelia relates to you 85%. Yet as a couple you are functioning perfectly, so you rightly begin to doubt the significance of the percentages I have given, thinking that with only 50% interest in your partner the marriage should not have lasted very long, whereas it has.

The explanation is simple and resides in the beauty of that surprising thing that is the bond of life, called *Love*... Love is the universal remedy for all indifference, against all difficulties. And even if it is your lot to suffer at times from a temporary loss of liberty, to deny yourself a certain pleasure, to restrict your personal comfort, you will have known how to transform this 50% into 70%, 80%, 90% or perhaps even 100% participation as a partner in this happy couple that you have created in the face of all odds. It is thus that the alchemist changes lead into gold—through Love and Sacrifice!

Another situation. You are still named Michael, and your wife is a Catherine. Our table of compatibilities is explicit, your situation is paradise! Michael–Catherine is 95% and Catherine–Michael is 95%. At the outset of your matrimonial adventure, all is euphoria, you are floating on a little pink cloud and then, a few months later, you are shipwrecked and meet your downfall. Why? Quite frankly, because you both believed that nothing could possibly go wrong, and that consequently no effort was necessary, that happiness was your due. And so it was that, just as in an abandoned garden wild plants spring up and choke the beautiful flowers, your union was undone by the selfishness that precedes indifference which, in its turn, leads to a debilitating boredom.

You can clearly ascertain how dangerous it is to trust in appearances and how one must be circumspect in the handling of compatibilities, for Providence always adds a new dimension to our judgements, and things are rarely as they seem.

In other words, whatever the percentages given to you, good or mediocre, never despair and equally never feel that you've got it made. The purpose of this little book is just to furnish you with some indications and tendencies. Nothing is certain in this lower world and the most dangerous battles, as we have seen, are those that seemed already won. A 95% may reassure you, of course, but also let it make you prudent. And do not let a 10% upset you, for it is the most doubtful combats that make the sweetest victories.

In life, there is really only one thing to fear, and that is surprise. It is this that brings the loss of battles, virtues, and the most desirable situations. It has often been said that a man forewarned is worth two. If this work enables you to be more attentive to the psychologies of others and more conscious of the image you project, I will have wasted neither my time nor yours.

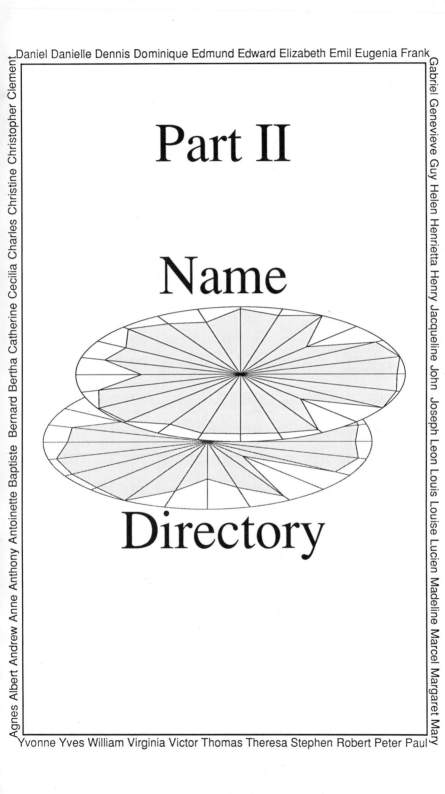

Part II

Name

Directory

Daniel Danielle Dennis Dominique Edmund Edward Elizabeth Emil Eugenia Frank

Gabriel Genevieve Guy Helen Henrietta Henry Jacqueline John Joseph Leon Louis Louise Lucien Madeline Marcel Margaret Mary

Agnes Albert Andrew Anne Anthony Antoinette Baptiste Bernard Bertha Catherine Cecilia Charles Christine Christopher Clement

Yvonne Yves William Virginia Victor Thomas Theresa Stephen Robert Peter Paul

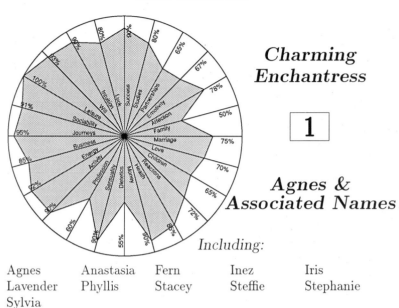

Charming Enchantress

1

Agnes & Associated Names

Including:

Agnes	Anastasia	Fern	Inez	Iris
Lavender	Phyllis	Stacey	Steffie	Stephanie
Sylvia				

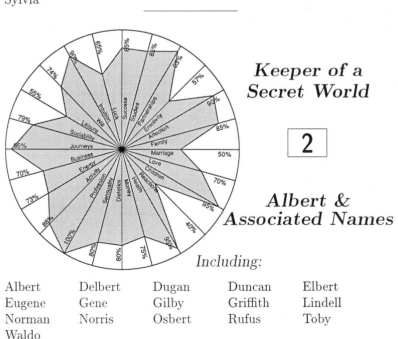

Keeper of a Secret World

2

Albert & Associated Names

Including:

Albert	Delbert	Dugan	Duncan	Elbert
Eugene	Gene	Gilby	Griffith	Lindell
Norman	Norris	Osbert	Rufus	Toby
Waldo				

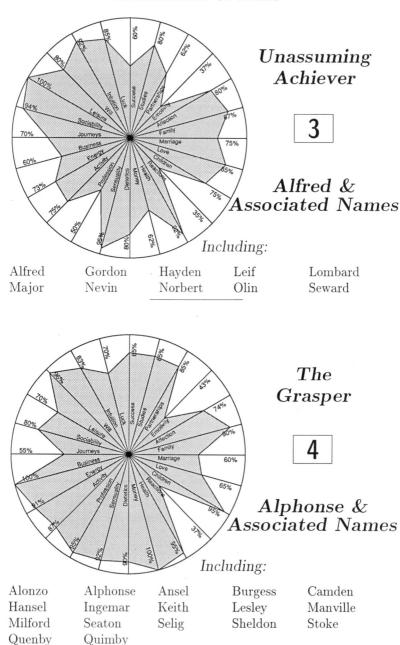

Unassuming Achiever

3

Alfred & Associated Names

Including:

Alfred	Gordon	Hayden	Leif	Lombard
Major	Nevin	Norbert	Olin	Seward

The Grasper

4

Alphonse & Associated Names

Including:

Alonzo	Alphonse	Ansel	Burgess	Camden
Hansel	Ingemar	Keith	Lesley	Manville
Milford	Seaton	Selig	Sheldon	Stoke
Quenby	Quimby			

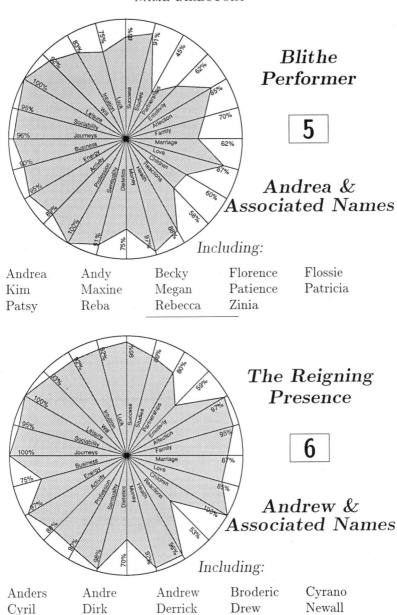

Blithe Performer

5

Andrea & Associated Names

Including:

Andrea	Andy	Becky	Florence	Flossie
Kim	Maxine	Megan	Patience	Patricia
Patsy	Reba	Rebecca	Zinia	

The Reigning Presence

6

Andrew & Associated Names

Including:

Anders	Andre	Andrew	Broderic	Cyrano
Cyril	Dirk	Derrick	Drew	Newall
Roscoe	Theodore	Tucker		

The Seeker of Experience

7

Anne & Associated Names

Including:

Alberta	Alexis	Amelia	Anita	Anne
Corinne	Emily	Ethel	Gwendolyn	Hanna
Lisa	Melissa	Nancy	Nina	Priscilla
Roxanne	Sandra	Tanya	Tory	Wendy

The Thinker

8

Anthony & Associated Names

Including:

Abbot	Anthony	Aristotle	Fabian	Harley
Kent	Lindsey	Oscar	Russell	Rusty
Taylor	Tony			

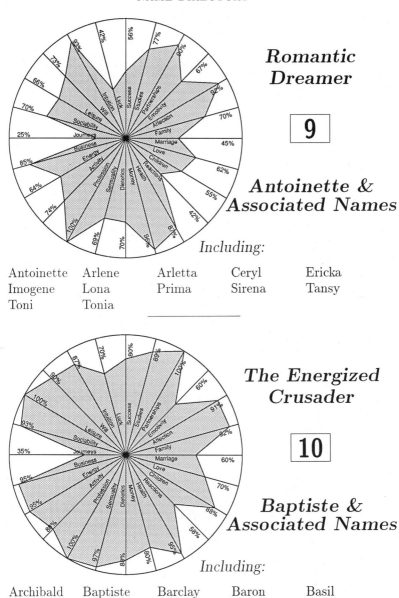

Romantic Dreamer

9

Antoinette & Associated Names

Including:

Antoinette	Arlene	Arletta	Ceryl	Ericka
Imogene	Lona	Prima	Sirena	Tansy
Toni	Tonia			

The Energized Crusader

10

Baptiste & Associated Names

Including:

Archibald	Baptiste	Barclay	Baron	Basil
Calvert	Cornelius	Floyd	Lloyd	Matthew
Neil	Ryan	Troy		

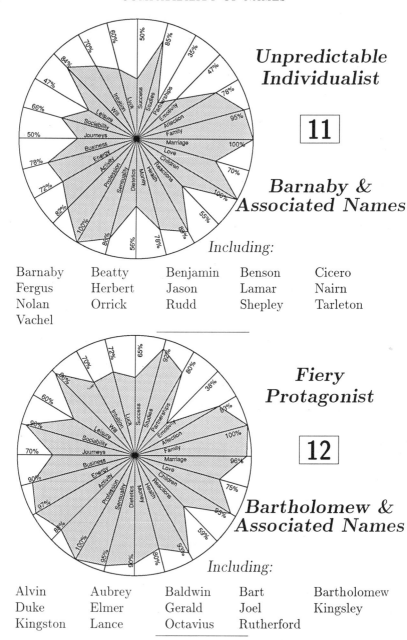

Unpredictable Individualist

11

Barnaby & Associated Names

Including:

Barnaby	Beatty	Benjamin	Benson	Cicero
Fergus	Herbert	Jason	Lamar	Nairn
Nolan	Orrick	Rudd	Shepley	Tarleton
Vachel				

Fiery Protagonist

12

Bartholomew & Associated Names

Including:

Alvin	Aubrey	Baldwin	Bart	Bartholomew
Duke	Elmer	Gerald	Joel	Kingsley
Kingston	Lance	Octavius	Rutherford	

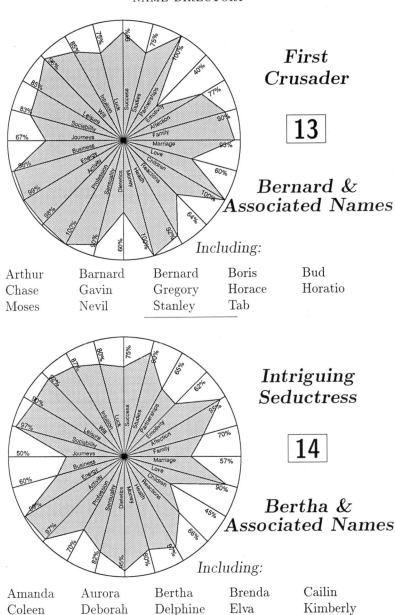

First Crusader

13

Bernard & Associated Names

Including:

Arthur	Barnard	Bernard	Boris	Bud
Chase	Gavin	Gregory	Horace	Horatio
Moses	Nevil	Stanley	Tab	

Intriguing Seductress

14

Bertha & Associated Names

Including:

Amanda	Aurora	Bertha	Brenda	Cailin
Coleen	Deborah	Delphine	Elva	Kimberly
Mandy	Melanie	Melinda	Millicent	Opal

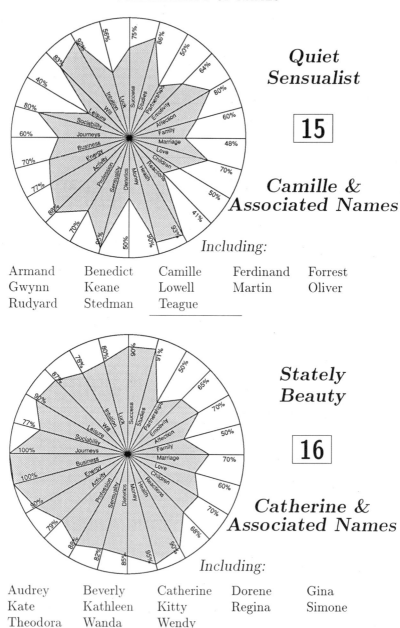

Quiet Sensualist

15

Camille & Associated Names

Including:

Armand	Benedict	Camille	Ferdinand	Forrest
Gwynn	Keane	Lowell	Martin	Oliver
Rudyard	Stedman	Teague		

Stately Beauty

16

Catherine & Associated Names

Including:

Audrey	Beverly	Catherine	Dorene	Gina
Kate	Kathleen	Kitty	Regina	Simone
Theodora	Wanda	Wendy		

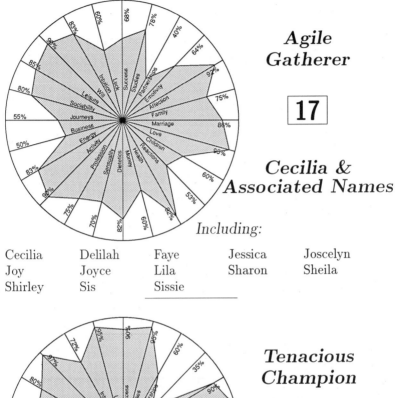

Agile Gatherer

17

Cecilia & Associated Names

Including:

Cecilia	Delilah	Faye	Jessica	Joscelyn
Joy	Joyce	Lila	Sharon	Sheila
Shirley	Sis	Sissie		

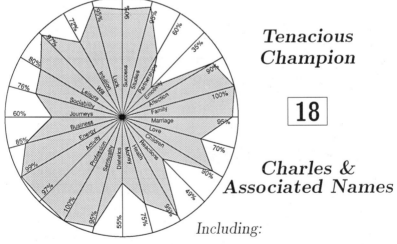

Tenacious Champion

18

Charles & Associated Names

Including:

Amos	Carl	Carlos	Charles	Colby
Gaylord	Jeremy	Jethro	Lester	Malcolm
Monroe	Nicholas	Nigel	Reed	Remington
Rochester	Saul	Sherman	Tracey	Winthrop

19

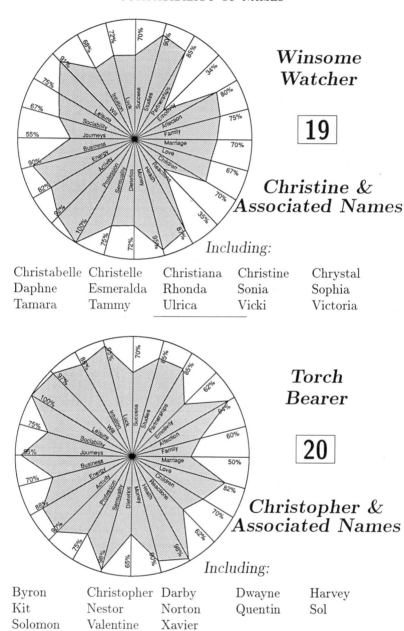

Winsome Watcher

19

Christine & Associated Names

Including:

Christabelle	Christelle	Christiana	Christine	Chrystal
Daphne	Esmeralda	Rhonda	Sonia	Sophia
Tamara	Tammy	Ulrica	Vicki	Victoria

Torch Bearer

20

Christopher & Associated Names

Including:

Byron	Christopher	Darby	Dwayne	Harvey
Kit	Nestor	Norton	Quentin	Sol
Solomon	Valentine	Xavier		

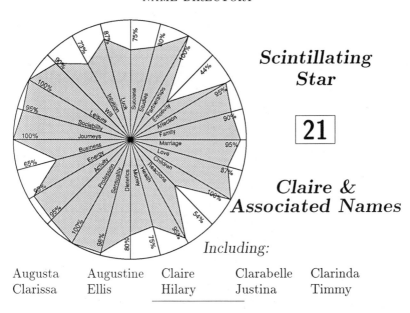

Scintillating Star

21

Claire & Associated Names

Including:

Augusta	Augustine	Claire	Clarabelle	Clarinda
Clarissa	Ellis	Hilary	Justina	Timmy

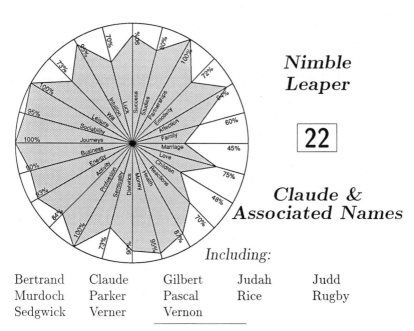

Nimble Leaper

22

Claude & Associated Names

Including:

Bertrand	Claude	Gilbert	Judah	Judd
Murdoch	Parker	Pascal	Rice	Rugby
Sedgwick	Verner	Vernon		

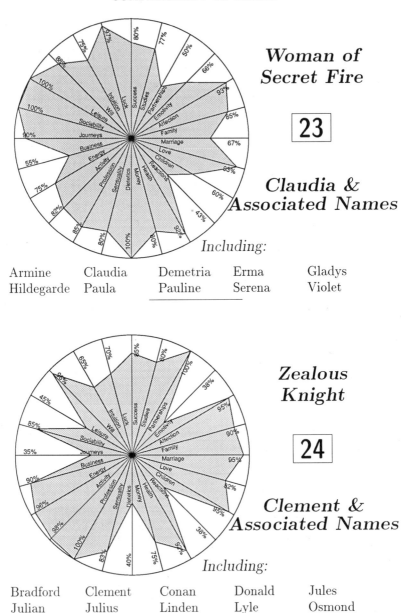

Woman of Secret Fire

23

Claudia & Associated Names

Including:

Armine	Claudia	Demetria	Erma	Gladys
Hildegarde	Paula	Pauline	Serena	Violet

Zealous Knight

24

Clement & Associated Names

Including:

Bradford	Clement	Conan	Donald	Jules
Julian	Julius	Linden	Lyle	Osmond
Perry	Riley	Squire	Uriel	

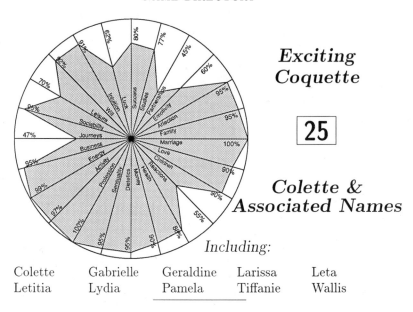

Exciting Coquette

25

Colette & Associated Names

Including:

Colette	Gabrielle	Geraldine	Larissa	Leta
Letitia	Lydia	Pamela	Tiffanie	Wallis

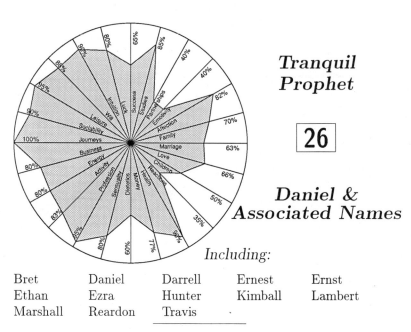

Tranquil Prophet

26

Daniel & Associated Names

Including:

Bret	Daniel	Darrell	Ernest	Ernst
Ethan	Ezra	Hunter	Kimball	Lambert
Marshall	Reardon	Travis		

23

Courier of Springtime

27

Danielle & Associated Names

Including:

Alfreda	Alva	Danielle	Delta	Elva
Eustacia	Kayla	Neva	Nevada	Pansy
Stacey				

Bringer of Unity and Joy

28

Denise & Associated Names

Including:

Adelpha	Argenta	Denise	Dixie	Fabienne
Jacinthia	Phaidra	Raphaela	Tallulah	Vashti
Zabrina				

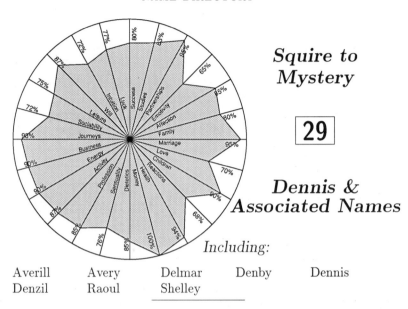

Squire to Mystery

29

Dennis & Associated Names

Including:

Averill	Avery	Delmar	Denby	Dennis
Denzil	Raoul	Shelley		

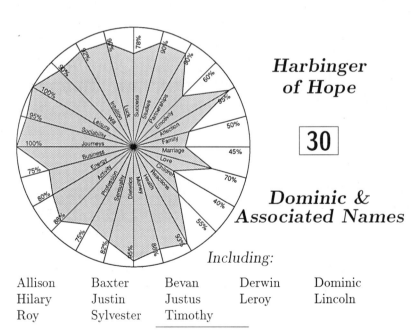

Harbinger of Hope

30

Dominic & Associated Names

Including:

Allison	Baxter	Bevan	Derwin	Dominic
Hilary	Justin	Justus	Leroy	Lincoln
Roy	Sylvester	Timothy		

25

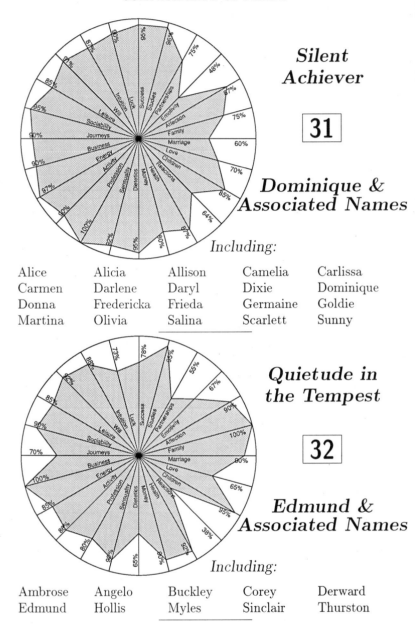

Silent Achiever

31

Dominique & Associated Names

Including:

Alice	Alicia	Allison	Camelia	Carlissa
Carmen	Darlene	Daryl	Dixie	Dominique
Donna	Fredericka	Frieda	Germaine	Goldie
Martina	Olivia	Salina	Scarlett	Sunny

Quietude in the Tempest

32

Edmund & Associated Names

Including:

Ambrose	Angelo	Buckley	Corey	Derward
Edmund	Hollis	Myles	Sinclair	Thurston

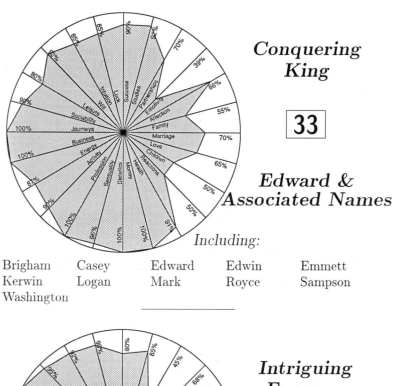

Conquering King

33

Edward & Associated Names

Including:

Brigham	Casey	Edward	Edwin	Emmett
Kerwin	Logan	Mark	Royce	Sampson
Washington				

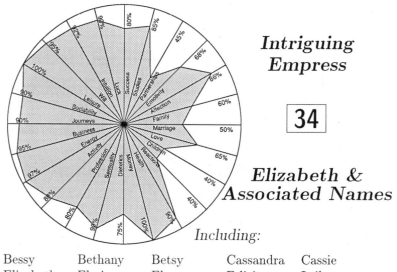

Intriguing Empress

34

Elizabeth & Associated Names

Including:

Bessy	Bethany	Betsy	Cassandra	Cassie
Elizabeth	Elmira	Elyse	Felicity	Leila
Leslie	Lilian	Lila	Lilac	Lily
Lisa				

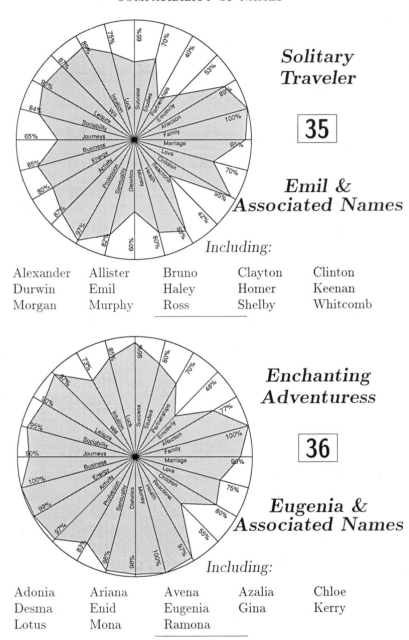

Solitary Traveler

35

Emil &
Associated Names

Including:

Alexander	Allister	Bruno	Clayton	Clinton
Durwin	Emil	Haley	Homer	Keenan
Morgan	Murphy	Ross	Shelby	Whitcomb

Enchanting Adventuress

36

Eugenia &
Associated Names

Including:

Adonia	Ariana	Avena	Azalia	Chloe
Desma	Enid	Eugenia	Gina	Kerry
Lotus	Mona	Ramona		

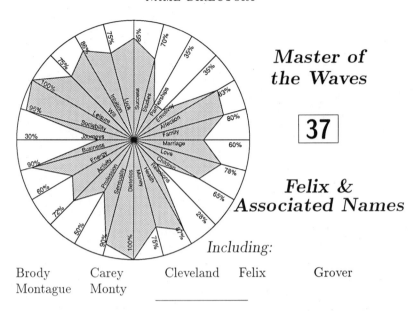

Master of the Waves

37

Felix & Associated Names

Including:

Brody	Carey	Cleveland	Felix	Grover
Montague	Monty			

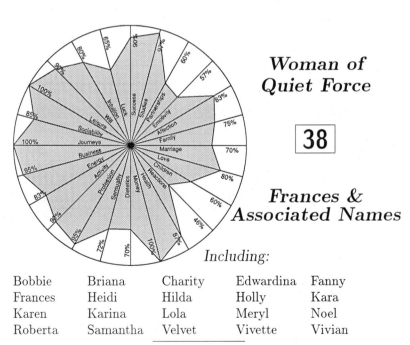

Woman of Quiet Force

38

Frances & Associated Names

Including:

Bobbie	Briana	Charity	Edwardina	Fanny
Frances	Heidi	Hilda	Holly	Kara
Karen	Karina	Lola	Meryl	Noel
Roberta	Samantha	Velvet	Vivette	Vivian

29

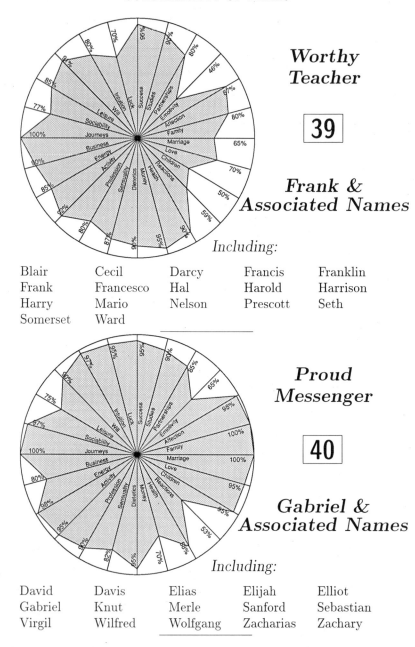

Worthy Teacher

39

Frank & Associated Names

Including:

Blair	Cecil	Darcy	Francis	Franklin
Frank	Francesco	Hal	Harold	Harrison
Harry	Mario	Nelson	Prescott	Seth
Somerset	Ward			

Proud Messenger

40

Gabriel & Associated Names

Including:

David	Davis	Elias	Elijah	Elliot
Gabriel	Knut	Merle	Sanford	Sebastian
Virgil	Wilfred	Wolfgang	Zacharias	Zachary

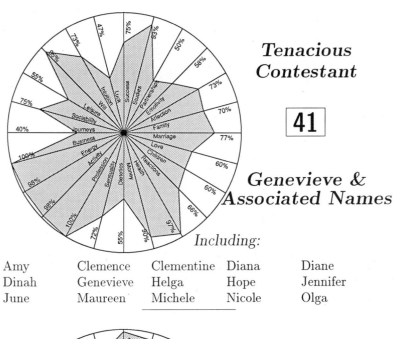

Tenacious Contestant

41

Genevieve & Associated Names

Including:

Amy	Clemence	Clementine	Diana	Diane
Dinah	Genevieve	Helga	Hope	Jennifer
June	Maureen	Michele	Nicole	Olga

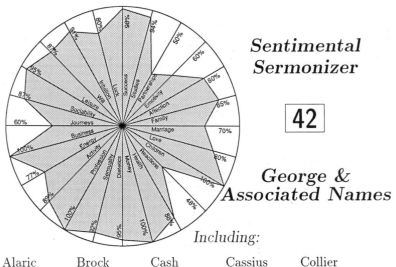

Sentimental Sermonizer

42

George & Associated Names

Including:

Alaric	Brock	Cash	Cassius	Collier
Corbett	Darren	Darrick	Desmond	Geoffrey
George	Igor	Jefferson	Jordan	Marvin
Mervin	Stacey	Woodrow		

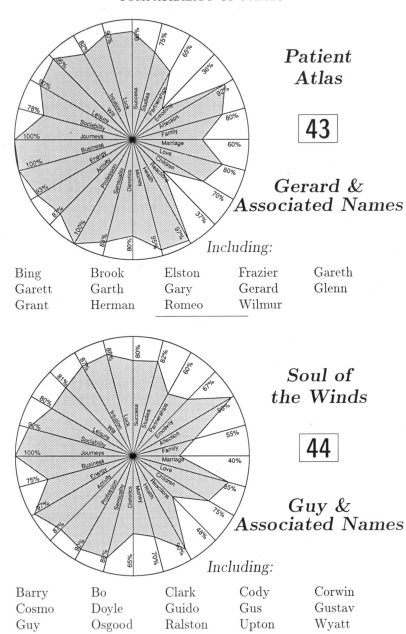

Patient Atlas

43

Gerard & Associated Names

Including:

Bing	Brook	Elston	Frazier	Gareth
Garett	Garth	Gary	Gerard	Glenn
Grant	Herman	Romeo	Wilmur	

Soul of the Winds

44

Guy & Associated Names

Including:

Barry	Bo	Clark	Cody	Corwin
Cosmo	Doyle	Guido	Gus	Gustav
Guy	Osgood	Ralston	Upton	Wyatt

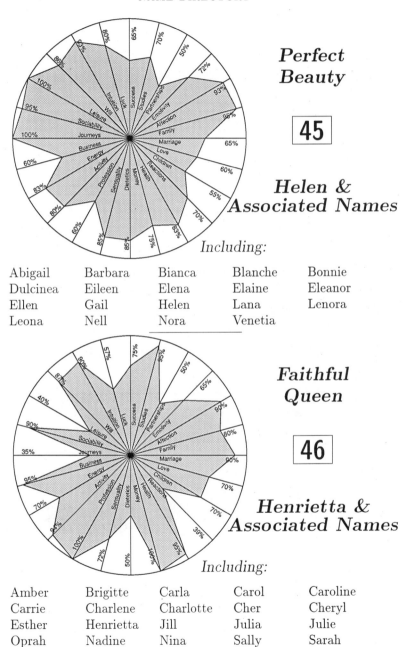

Perfect Beauty

45

Helen & Associated Names

Including:

Abigail	Barbara	Bianca	Blanche	Bonnie
Dulcinea	Eileen	Elena	Elaine	Eleanor
Ellen	Gail	Helen	Lana	Lenora
Leona	Nell	Nora	Venetia	

Faithful Queen

46

Henrietta & Associated Names

Including:

Amber	Brigitte	Carla	Carol	Caroline
Carrie	Charlene	Charlotte	Cher	Cheryl
Esther	Henrietta	Jill	Julia	Julie
Oprah	Nadine	Nina	Sally	Sarah

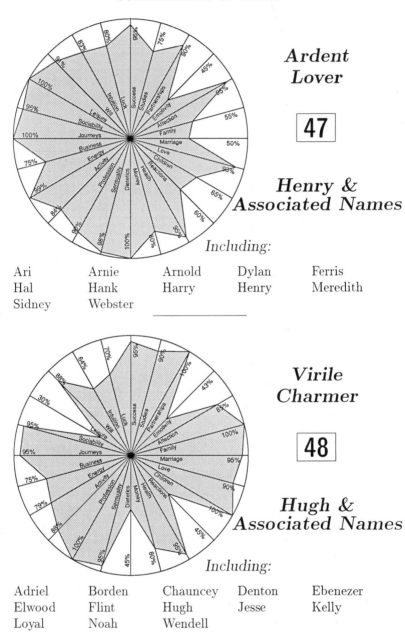

Ardent Lover

$$\boxed{47}$$

Henry & Associated Names

Including:

Ari	Arnie	Arnold	Dylan	Ferris
Hal	Hank	Harry	Henry	Meredith
Sidney	Webster			

Virile Charmer

$$\boxed{48}$$

Hugh & Associated Names

Including:

Adriel	Borden	Chauncey	Denton	Ebenezer
Elwood	Flint	Hugh	Jesse	Kelly
Loyal	Noah	Wendell		

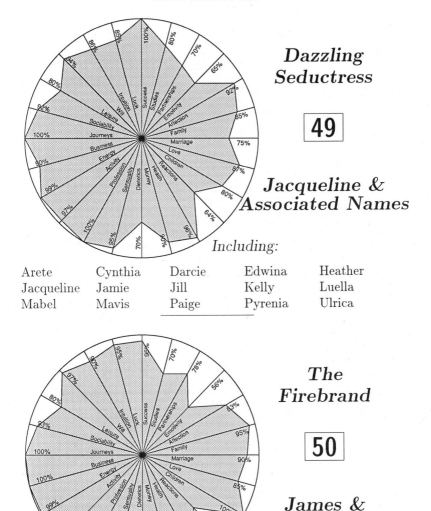

Dazzling Seductress

49

Jacqueline & Associated Names

Including:

Arete	Cynthia	Darcie	Edwina	Heather
Jacqueline	Jamie	Jill	Kelly	Luella
Mabel	Mavis	Paige	Pyrenia	Ulrica

The Firebrand

50

James & Associated Names

Including:

Burton	Channing	Cleeve	Clifford	Cooper
Damien	Earl	Elton	Errol	Gerome
Jackson	Jacob	Jake	James	Jock
Percy	Reginald	Ronald	Stuart	Zeke

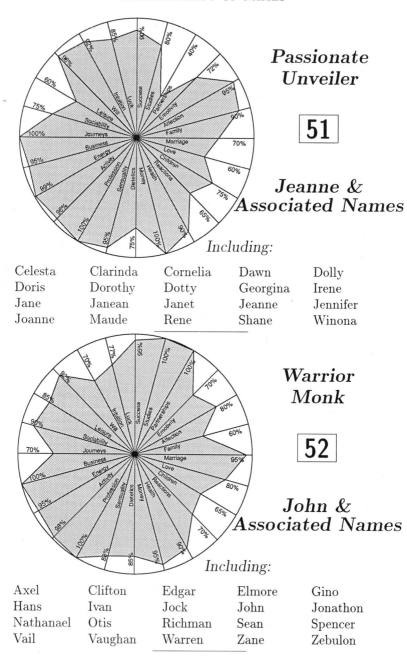

Passionate Unveiler

51

Jeanne & Associated Names

Including:

Celesta	Clarinda	Cornelia	Dawn	Dolly
Doris	Dorothy	Dotty	Georgina	Irene
Jane	Janean	Janet	Jeanne	Jennifer
Joanne	Maude	Rene	Shane	Winona

Warrior Monk

52

John & Associated Names

Including:

Axel	Clifton	Edgar	Elmore	Gino
Hans	Ivan	Jock	John	Jonathon
Nathanael	Otis	Richman	Sean	Spencer
Vail	Vaughan	Warren	Zane	Zebulon

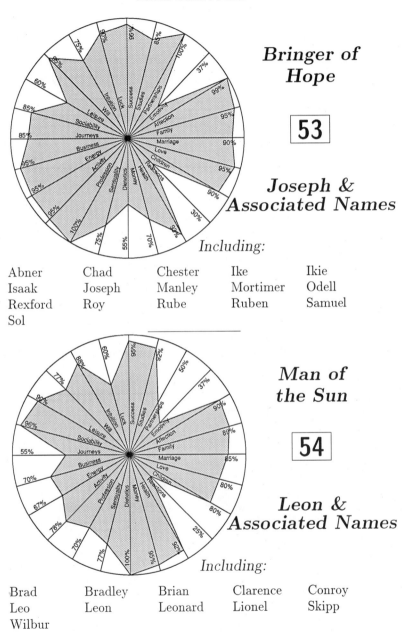

Bringer of Hope

53

Joseph & Associated Names

Including:

Abner	Chad	Chester	Ike	Ikie
Isaak	Joseph	Manley	Mortimer	Odell
Rexford	Roy	Rube	Ruben	Samuel
Sol				

Man of the Sun

54

Leon & Associated Names

Including:

Brad	Bradley	Brian	Clarence	Conroy
Leo	Leon	Leonard	Lionel	Skipp
Wilbur				

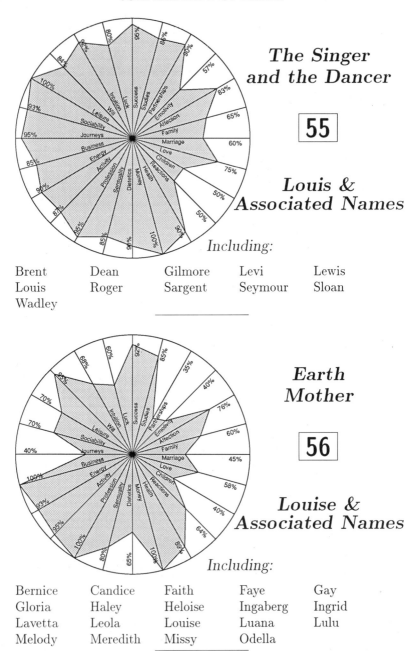

The Singer and the Dancer

55

Louis & Associated Names

Including:

Brent	Dean	Gilmore	Levi	Lewis
Louis	Roger	Sargent	Seymour	Sloan
Wadley				

Earth Mother

56

Louise & Associated Names

Including:

Bernice	Candice	Faith	Faye	Gay
Gloria	Haley	Heloise	Ingaberg	Ingrid
Lavetta	Leola	Louise	Luana	Lulu
Melody	Meredith	Missy	Odella	

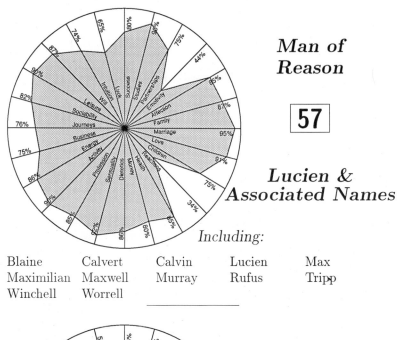

Man of Reason

57

Lucien & Associated Names

Including:

Blaine	Calvert	Calvin	Lucien	Max
Maximilian	Maxwell	Murray	Rufus	Tripp
Winchell	Worrell			

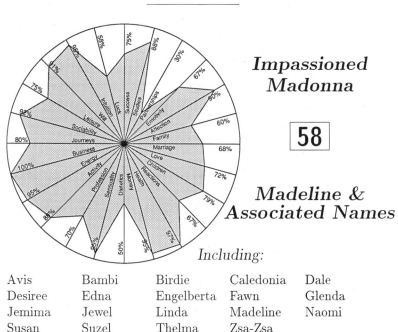

Impassioned Madonna

58

Madeline & Associated Names

Including:

Avis	Bambi	Birdie	Caledonia	Dale
Desiree	Edna	Engelberta	Fawn	Glenda
Jemima	Jewel	Linda	Madeline	Naomi
Susan	Suzel	Thelma	Zsa-Zsa	

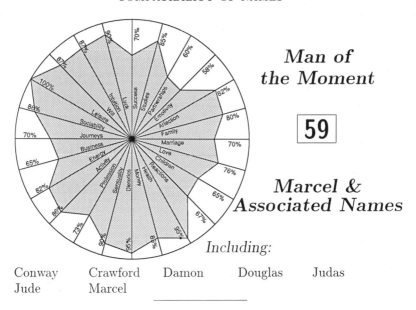

Man of the Moment

59

Marcel & Associated Names

Including:

Conway	Crawford	Damon	Douglas	Judas
Jude	Marcel			

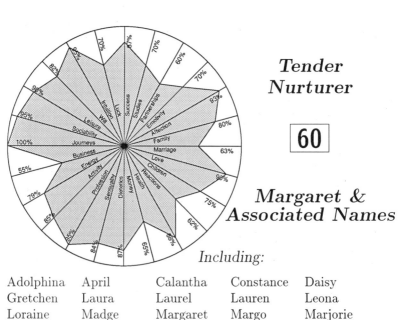

Tender Nurturer

60

Margaret & Associated Names

Including:

Adolphina	April	Calantha	Constance	Daisy
Gretchen	Laura	Laurel	Lauren	Leona
Loraine	Madge	Margaret	Margo	Marjorie
Pearl	Peggy	Rita	Rowena	

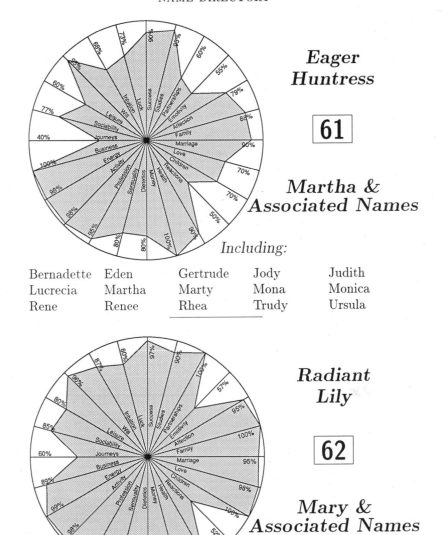

Eager Huntress

61

Martha & Associated Names

Including:

Bernadette	Eden	Gertrude	Jody	Judith
Lucrecia	Martha	Marty	Mona	Monica
Rene	Renee	Rhea	Trudy	Ursula

Radiant Lily

62

Mary & Associated Names

Including:

Beatrice	Eva	Evelyn	Grace	Gwenn
Marilyn	Marlene	Mary	Maryanne	Maureen
Molly	Morgan	Muriel	Norma	Ruth
Selma	Trixie	Vanna	Vanessa	Veronica

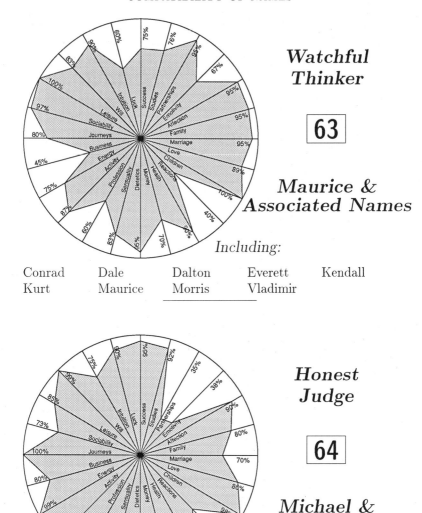

Watchful Thinker

63

Maurice & Associated Names

Including:

Conrad	Dale	Dalton	Everett	Kendall
Kurt	Maurice	Morris	Vladimir	

Honest Judge

64

Michael & Associated Names

Including:

Adam	Dick	Ellery	Hardy	Michael
Micky	Mitchell	Napoleon	Richard	Vito
Welby				

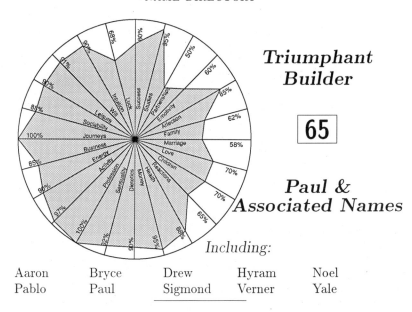

Triumphant Builder

65

Paul & Associated Names

Including:

Aaron	Bryce	Drew	Hyram	Noel
Pablo	Paul	Sigmond	Verner	Yale

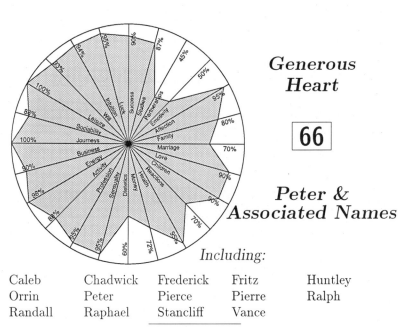

Generous Heart

66

Peter & Associated Names

Including:

Caleb	Chadwick	Frederick	Fritz	Huntley
Orrin	Peter	Pierce	Pierre	Ralph
Randall	Raphael	Stancliff	Vance	

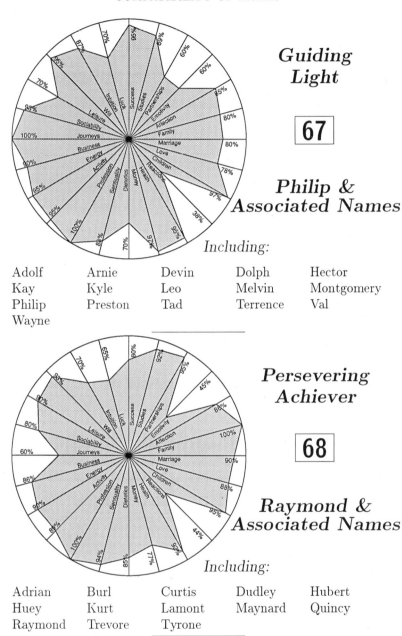

Guiding Light

67

Philip & Associated Names

Including:

Adolf	Arnie	Devin	Dolph	Hector
Kay	Kyle	Leo	Melvin	Montgomery
Philip	Preston	Tad	Terrence	Val
Wayne				

Persevering Achiever

68

Raymond & Associated Names

Including:

Adrian	Burl	Curtis	Dudley	Hubert
Huey	Kurt	Lamont	Maynard	Quincy
Raymond	Trevore	Tyrone		

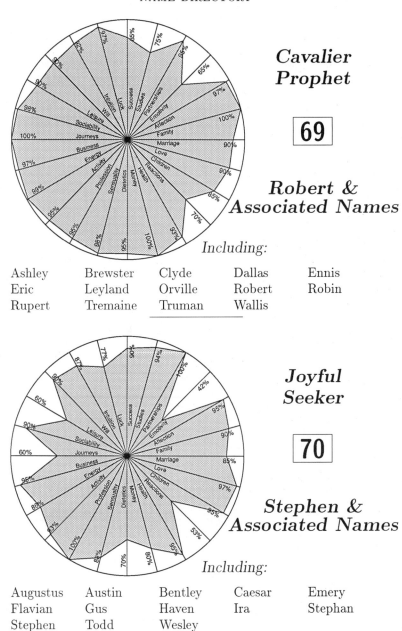

Cavalier Prophet

69

Robert & Associated Names

Including:

Ashley	Brewster	Clyde	Dallas	Ennis
Eric	Leyland	Orville	Robert	Robin
Rupert	Tremaine	Truman	Wallis	

Joyful Seeker

70

Stephen & Associated Names

Including:

Augustus	Austin	Bentley	Caesar	Emery
Flavian	Gus	Haven	Ira	Stephan
Stephen	Todd	Wesley		

Bearer of Good Fortune

71

Theresa & Associated Names

Including:

Aurora	Brooke	Deane	Edda	Eleanor
Emmaline	Hazel	Leah	Leana	Lenora
Lucille	Marcy	Marsha	Rachel	Rae
Shelley	Tara	Teri	Theresa	Tracey

The Sower and the Reaper

72

Thomas & Associated Names

Including:

Adlai	Allan	Bruce	Cameron	Derrick
Dirk	Dolph	Enos	Graham	Joshua
Robinson	Rudolf	Thomas		

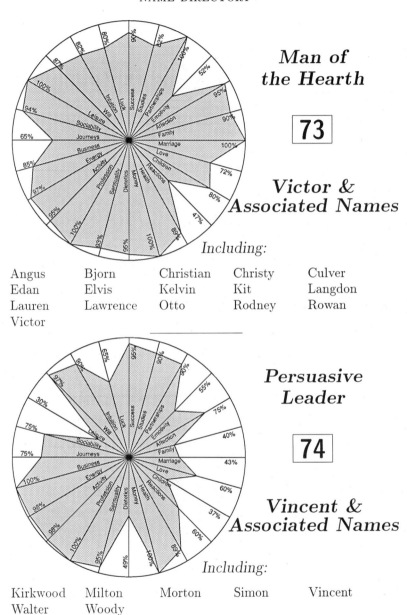

Man of the Hearth

73

Victor & Associated Names

Including:

Angus	Bjorn	Christian	Christy	Culver
Edan	Elvis	Kelvin	Kit	Langdon
Lauren	Lawrence	Otto	Rodney	Rowan
Victor				

Persuasive Leader

74

Vincent & Associated Names

Including:

Kirkwood	Milton	Morton	Simon	Vincent
Walter	Woody			

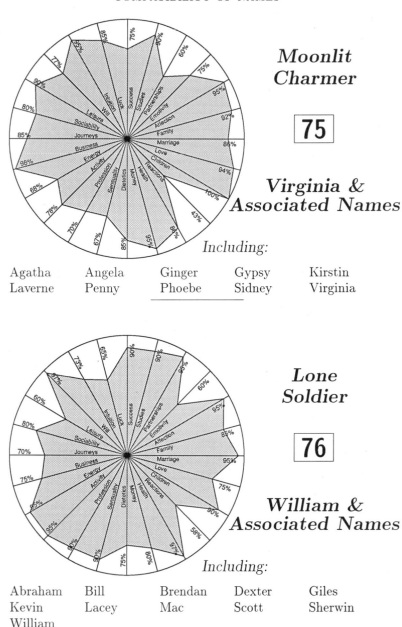

Moonlit Charmer

75

Virginia & Associated Names

Including:

Agatha	Angela	Ginger	Gypsy	Kirstin
Laverne	Penny	Phoebe	Sidney	Virginia

Lone Soldier

76

William & Associated Names

Including:

Abraham	Bill	Brendan	Dexter	Giles
Kevin	Lacey	Mac	Scott	Sherwin
William				

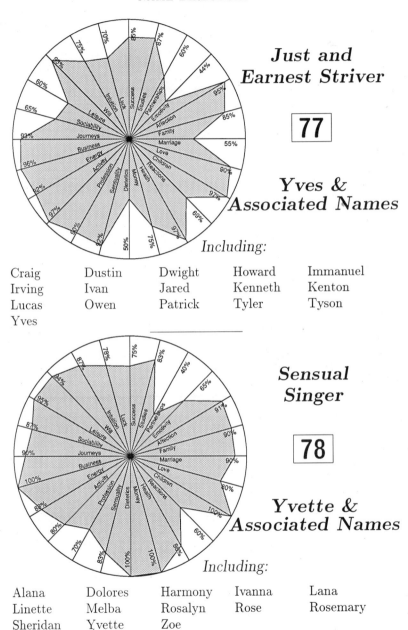

Just and Earnest Striver

77

Yves & Associated Names

Including:

Craig	Dustin	Dwight	Howard	Immanuel
Irving	Ivan	Jared	Kenneth	Kenton
Lucas	Owen	Patrick	Tyler	Tyson
Yves				

Sensual Singer

78

Yvette & Associated Names

Including:

Alana	Dolores	Harmony	Ivanna	Lana
Linette	Melba	Rosalyn	Rose	Rosemary
Sheridan	Yvette	Zoe		

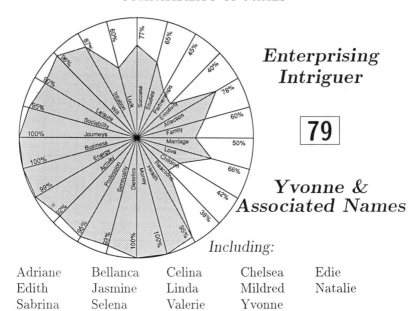

Enterprising Intriguer

79

Yvonne & Associated Names

Including:

Adriane	Bellanca	Celina	Chelsea	Edie
Edith	Jasmine	Linda	Mildred	Natalie
Sabrina	Selena	Valerie	Yvonne	

INDEX OF POPULAR NAMES
(For a complete list of 9000 names refer to *The Name Book*)

(For a complete list of 9000 names refer to *The Name Book*)

47	Arnie, *p.* 34	79	Bellanca, *p.* 50
47	Arnold, *p.* 34	15	Benedict, *p.* 18
13	Arthur, *p.* 17	11	Benjamin, *p.* 16
69	Ashley, *p.* 45	11	Benson, *p.* 16
12	Aubrey, *p.* 16	70	Bentley, *p.* 45
16	Audrey, *p.* 18	61	Bernadette, *p.* 41
21	Augusta, *p.* 21	13	Bernard, *p.* 17
21	Augustine, *p.* 21	56	Bernice, *p.* 38
70	Augustus, *p.* 45	14	Bertha, *p.* 17
71	Aurora, *p.* 46	22	Bertrand, *p.* 21
14	Aurora, *p.* 17	34	Bessy, *p.* 27
70	Austin, *p.* 45	34	Bethany, *p.* 27
36	Avena, *p.* 28	34	Betsy, *p.* 27
29	Averill, *p.* 25	30	Bevan, *p.* 25
29	Avery, *p.* 25	16	Beverly, *p.* 18
58	Avis, *p.* 39	45	Bianca, *p.* 33
52	Axel, *p.* 36	76	Bill, *p.* 48
36	Azalia, *p.* 28	43	Bing, *p.* 32
12	Baldwin, *p.* 16	58	Birdie, *p.* 39
58	Bambi, *p.* 39	73	Bjorn, *p.* 47
10	Baptiste, *p.* 15	57	Blaine, *p.* 39
45	Barbara, *p.* 33	39	Blair, *p.* 30
10	Barclay, *p.* 15	45	Blanche, *p.* 33
11	Barnaby, *p.* 16	44	Bo, *p.* 32
13	Barnard, *p.* 17	38	Bobbie, *p.* 29
10	Baron, *p.* 15	45	Bonnie, *p.* 33
44	Barry, *p.* 32	48	Borden, *p.* 34
12	Bart, *p.* 16	13	Boris, *p.* 17
12	Bartholomew, *p.* 16	54	Brad, *p.* 37
10	Basil, *p.* 15	24	Bradford, *p.* 22
30	Baxter, *p.* 25	54	Bradley, *p.* 37
62	Beatrice, *p.* 41	14	Brenda, *p.* 17
11	Beatty, *p.* 16	76	Brendan, *p.* 48
5	Becky, *p.* 13	55	Brent, *p.* 38

(For a complete list of 9000 names refer to *The Name Book*)

26	Bret, *p.* 23	18	Carl, *p.* 19
69	Brewster, *p.* 45	46	Carla, *p.* 33
54	Brian, *p.* 37	31	Carlissa, *p.* 26
38	Briana, *p.* 29	18	Carlos, *p.* 19
33	Brigham, *p.* 27	31	Carmen, *p.* 26
46	Brigitte, *p.* 33	46	Carol, *p.* 33
42	Brock, *p.* 31	46	Caroline, *p.* 33
6	Broderic, *p.* 13	46	Carrie, *p.* 33
37	Brody, *p.* 29	33	Casey, *p.* 27
43	Brook, *p.* 32	42	Cash, *p.* 31
71	Brooke, *p.* 46	34	Cassandra, *p.* 27
72	Bruce, *p.* 46	34	Cassie, *p.* 27
35	Bruno, *p.* 28	42	Cassius, *p.* 31
65	Bryce, *p.* 43	16	Catherine, *p.* 18
32	Buckley, *p.* 26	39	Cecil, *p.* 30
13	Bud, *p.* 17	17	Cecilia, *p.* 19
4	Burgess, *p.* 12	51	Celesta, *p.* 36
68	Burl, *p.* 44	79	Celina, *p.* 50
50	Burton, *p.* 35	9	Ceryl, *p.* 15
20	Byron, *p.* 20	53	Chad, *p.* 37
70	Caesar, *p.* 45	66	Chadwick, *p.* 43
14	Cailin, *p.* 17	50	Channing, *p.* 35
60	Calantha, *p.* 40	38	Charity, *p.* 29
66	Caleb, *p.* 43	46	Charlene, *p.* 33
58	Caledonia, *p.* 39	18	Charles, *p.* 19
57	Calvert, *p.* 39	46	Charlotte, *p.* 33
10	Calvert, *p.* 15	13	Chase, *p.* 17
57	Calvin, *p.* 39	48	Chauncey, *p.* 34
4	Camden, *p.* 12	79	Chelsea, *p.* 50
31	Camelia, *p.* 26	46	Cher, *p.* 33
72	Cameron, *p.* 46	46	Cheryl, *p.* 33
15	Camille, *p.* 18	53	Chester, *p.* 37
56	Candice, *p.* 38	36	Chloe, *p.* 28
37	Carey, *p.* 29	19	Christabelle, *p.* 20

(For a complete list of 9000 names refer to *The Name Book*)

19 Christelle, *p.* 20	54 Conroy, *p.* 37
73 Christian, *p.* 47	60 Constance, *p.* 40
19 Christiana, *p.* 20	59 Conway, *p.* 40
19 Christine, *p.* 20	50 Cooper, *p.* 35
20 Christopher, *p.* 20	42 Corbett, *p.* 31
73 Christy, *p.* 47	32 Corey, *p.* 26
19 Chrystal, *p.* 20	7 Corinne, *p.* 14
11 Cicero, *p.* 16	51 Cornelia, *p.* 36
21 Claire, *p.* 21	10 Cornelius, *p.* 15
21 Clarabelle, *p.* 21	44 Corwin, *p.* 32
54 Clarence, *p.* 37	44 Cosmo, *p.* 32
51 Clarinda, *p.* 36	77 Craig, *p.* 49
21 Clarinda, *p.* 21	59 Crawford, *p.* 40
21 Clarissa, *p.* 21	73 Culver, *p.* 47
44 Clark, *p.* 32	68 Curtis, *p.* 44
22 Claude, *p.* 21	49 Cynthia, *p.* 35
23 Claudia, *p.* 22	6 Cyrano, *p.* 13
35 Clayton, *p.* 28	6 Cyril, *p.* 13
50 Cleeve, *p.* 35	60 Daisy, *p.* 40
41 Clemence, *p.* 31	63 Dale, *p.* 42
24 Clement, *p.* 22	58 Dale, *p.* 39
41 Clementine, *p.* 31	69 Dallas, *p.* 45
37 Cleveland, *p.* 29	63 Dalton, *p.* 42
50 Clifford, *p.* 35	50 Damien, *p.* 35
52 Clifton, *p.* 36	59 Damon, *p.* 40
35 Clinton, *p.* 28	26 Daniel, *p.* 23
69 Clyde, *p.* 45	27 Danielle, *p.* 24
44 Cody, *p.* 32	19 Daphne, *p.* 20
18 Colby, *p.* 19	20 Darby, *p.* 20
14 Coleen, *p.* 17	49 Darcie, *p.* 35
25 Colette, *p.* 23	39 Darcy, *p.* 30
42 Collier, *p.* 31	31 Darlene, *p.* 26
24 Conan, *p.* 22	26 Darrell, *p.* 23
63 Conrad, *p.* 42	42 Darren, *p.* 31

(For a complete list of 9000 names refer to _The Name Book_)

42 Darrick, _p._ 31	31 Dixie, _p._ 26
31 Daryl, _p._ 26	28 Dixie, _p._ 24
40 David, _p._ 30	51 Dolly, _p._ 36
40 Davis, _p._ 30	78 Dolores, _p._ 49
51 Dawn, _p._ 36	72 Dolph, _p._ 46
55 Dean, _p._ 38	67 Dolph, _p._ 44
71 Deane, _p._ 46	30 Dominic, _p._ 25
14 Deborah, _p._ 17	31 Dominique, _p._ 26
2 Delbert, _p._ 11	24 Donald, _p._ 22
17 Delilah, _p._ 19	31 Donna, _p._ 26
29 Delmar, _p._ 25	16 Dorene, _p._ 18
14 Delphine, _p._ 17	51 Doris, _p._ 36
27 Delta, _p._ 24	51 Dorothy, _p._ 36
23 Demetria, _p._ 22	51 Dotty, _p._ 36
29 Denby, _p._ 25	59 Douglas, _p._ 40
28 Denise, _p._ 24	44 Doyle, _p._ 32
29 Dennis, _p._ 25	65 Drew, _p._ 43
48 Denton, _p._ 34	6 Drew, _p._ 13
29 Denzil, _p._ 25	68 Dudley, _p._ 44
72 Derrick, _p._ 46	2 Dugan, _p._ 11
6 Derrick, _p._ 13	12 Duke, _p._ 16
32 Derward, _p._ 26	45 Dulcinea, _p._ 33
30 Derwin, _p._ 25	2 Duncan, _p._ 11
58 Desiree, _p._ 39	35 Durwin, _p._ 28
36 Desma, _p._ 28	77 Dustin, _p._ 49
42 Desmond, _p._ 31	20 Dwayne, _p._ 20
67 Devin, _p._ 44	77 Dwight, _p._ 49
76 Dexter, _p._ 48	47 Dylan, _p._ 34
41 Diana, _p._ 31	50 Earl, _p._ 35
41 Diane, _p._ 31	48 Ebenezer, _p._ 34
64 Dick, _p._ 42	73 Edan, _p._ 47
41 Dinah, _p._ 31	71 Edda, _p._ 46
72 Dirk, _p._ 46	61 Eden, _p._ 41
6 Dirk, _p._ 13	52 Edgar, _p._ 36

(For a complete list of 9000 names refer to *The Name Book*)

79	Edie, p. 50	71	Emmaline, p. 46
79	Edith, p. 50	33	Emmett, p. 27
32	Edmund, p. 26	58	Engelberta, p. 39
58	Edna, p. 39	36	Enid, p. 28
33	Edward, p. 27	69	Ennis, p. 45
38	Edwardina, p. 29	72	Enos, p. 46
33	Edwin, p. 27	69	Eric, p. 45
49	Edwina, p. 35	9	Ericka, p. 15
45	Eileen, p. 33	23	Erma, p. 22
45	Elaine, p. 33	26	Ernest, p. 23
2	Elbert, p. 11	26	Ernst, p. 23
71	Eleanor, p. 46	50	Errol, p. 35
45	Eleanor, p. 33	19	Esmeralda, p. 20
45	Elena, p. 33	46	Esther, p. 33
40	Elias, p. 30	26	Ethan, p. 23
40	Elijah, p. 30	7	Ethel, p. 14
34	Elizabeth, p. 27	2	Eugene, p. 11
45	Ellen, p. 33	36	Eugenia, p. 28
64	Ellery, p. 42	27	Eustacia, p. 24
40	Elliot, p. 30	62	Eva, p. 41
21	Ellis, p. 21	62	Evelyn, p. 41
12	Elmer, p. 16	63	Everett, p. 42
34	Elmira, p. 27	26	Ezra, p. 23
52	Elmore, p. 36	8	Fabian, p. 14
43	Elston, p. 32	28	Fabienne, p. 24
50	Elton, p. 35	56	Faith, p. 38
27	Elva, p. 24	38	Fanny, p. 29
14	Elva, p. 17	58	Fawn, p. 39
73	Elvis, p. 47	56	Faye, p. 38
48	Elwood, p. 34	17	Faye, p. 19
34	Elyse, p. 27	34	Felicity, p. 27
70	Emery, p. 45	37	Felix, p. 29
35	Emil, p. 28	15	Ferdinand, p. 18
7	Emily, p. 14	11	Fergus, p. 16

(For a complete list of 9000 names refer to *The Name Book*)

1	Fern, *p.* 11	25	Geraldine, *p.* 23
47	Ferris, *p.* 34	43	Gerard, *p.* 32
70	Flavian, *p.* 45	31	Germaine, *p.* 26
48	Flint, *p.* 34	50	Gerome, *p.* 35
5	Florence, *p.* 13	61	Gertrude, *p.* 41
5	Flossie, *p.* 13	22	Gilbert, *p.* 21
10	Floyd, *p.* 15	2	Gilby, *p.* 11
15	Forrest, *p.* 18	76	Giles, *p.* 48
38	Frances, *p.* 29	55	Gilmore, *p.* 38
39	Francesco, *p.* 30	36	Gina, *p.* 28
39	Francis, *p.* 30	16	Gina, *p.* 18
39	Frank, *p.* 30	75	Ginger, *p.* 48
39	Franklin, *p.* 30	52	Gino, *p.* 36
43	Frazier, *p.* 32	23	Gladys, *p.* 22
66	Frederick, *p.* 43	58	Glenda, *p.* 39
31	Fredericka, *p.* 26	43	Glenn, *p.* 32
31	Frieda, *p.* 26	56	Gloria, *p.* 38
66	Fritz, *p.* 43	31	Goldie, *p.* 26
40	Gabriel, *p.* 30	3	Gordon, *p.* 12
25	Gabrielle, *p.* 23	62	Grace, *p.* 41
45	Gail, *p.* 33	72	Graham, *p.* 46
43	Gareth, *p.* 32	43	Grant, *p.* 32
43	Garett, *p.* 32	13	Gregory, *p.* 17
43	Garth, *p.* 32	60	Gretchen, *p.* 40
43	Gary, *p.* 32	2	Griffith, *p.* 11
13	Gavin, *p.* 17	37	Grover, *p.* 29
56	Gay, *p.* 38	44	Guido, *p.* 32
18	Gaylord, *p.* 19	70	Gus, *p.* 45
2	Gene, *p.* 11	44	Gus, *p.* 32
41	Genevieve, *p.* 31	44	Gustav, *p.* 32
42	Geoffrey, *p.* 31	44	Guy, *p.* 32
42	George, *p.* 31	7	Gwendolyn, *p.* 14
51	Georgina, *p.* 36	62	Gwenn, *p.* 41
12	Gerald, *p.* 16	15	Gwynn, *p.* 18

(For a complete list of 9000 names refer to *The Name Book*)

75	Gypsy, *p.* 48	32	Hollis, *p.* 26
47	Hal, *p.* 34	38	Holly, *p.* 29
39	Hal, *p.* 30	35	Homer, *p.* 28
56	Haley, *p.* 38	41	Hope, *p.* 31
35	Haley, *p.* 28	13	Horace, *p.* 17
47	Hank, *p.* 34	13	Horatio, *p.* 17
7	Hanna, *p.* 14	77	Howard, *p.* 49
52	Hans, *p.* 36	68	Hubert, *p.* 44
4	Hansel, *p.* 12	68	Huey, *p.* 44
64	Hardy, *p.* 42	48	Hugh, *p.* 34
8	Harley, *p.* 14	26	Hunter, *p.* 23
78	Harmony, *p.* 49	66	Huntley, *p.* 43
39	Harold, *p.* 30	65	Hyram, *p.* 43
39	Harrison, *p.* 30	42	Igor, *p.* 31
47	Harry, *p.* 34	53	Ike, *p.* 37
39	Harry, *p.* 30	53	Ikie, *p.* 37
20	Harvey, *p.* 20	77	Immanuel, *p.* 49
70	Haven, *p.* 45	9	Imogene, *p.* 15
3	Hayden, *p.* 12	1	Inez, *p.* 11
71	Hazel, *p.* 46	56	Ingaberg, *p.* 38
49	Heather, *p.* 35	4	Ingemar, *p.* 12
67	Hector, *p.* 44	56	Ingrid, *p.* 38
38	Heidi, *p.* 29	70	Ira, *p.* 45
45	Helen, *p.* 33	51	Irene, *p.* 36
41	Helga, *p.* 31	1	Iris, *p.* 11
56	Heloise, *p.* 38	77	Irving, *p.* 49
46	Henrietta, *p.* 33	53	Isaak, *p.* 37
47	Henry, *p.* 34	77	Ivan, *p.* 49
11	Herbert, *p.* 16	52	Ivan, *p.* 36
43	Herman, *p.* 32	78	Ivanna, *p.* 49
30	Hilary, *p.* 25	28	Jacinthia, *p.* 24
21	Hilary, *p.* 21	50	Jackson, *p.* 35
38	Hilda, *p.* 29	50	Jacob, *p.* 35
23	Hildegarde, *p.* 22	49	Jacqueline, *p.* 35

(For a complete list of 9000 names refer to *The Name Book*)

50	Jake, *p.* 35	22	Judah, *p.* 21
50	James, *p.* 35	59	Judas, *p.* 40
49	Jamie, *p.* 35	22	Judd, *p.* 21
51	Jane, *p.* 36	59	Jude, *p.* 40
51	Janean, *p.* 36	61	Judith, *p.* 41
51	Janet, *p.* 36	24	Jules, *p.* 22
77	Jared, *p.* 49	46	Julia, *p.* 33
79	Jasmine, *p.* 50	24	Julian, *p.* 22
11	Jason, *p.* 16	46	Julie, *p.* 33
51	Jeanne, *p.* 36	24	Julius, *p.* 22
42	Jefferson, *p.* 31	41	June, *p.* 31
58	Jemima, *p.* 39	30	Justin, *p.* 25
51	Jennifer, *p.* 36	21	Justina, *p.* 21
41	Jennifer, *p.* 31	30	Justus, *p.* 25
18	Jeremy, *p.* 19	38	Kara, *p.* 29
48	Jesse, *p.* 34	38	Karen, *p.* 29
17	Jessica, *p.* 19	38	Karina, *p.* 29
18	Jethro, *p.* 19	16	Kate, *p.* 18
58	Jewel, *p.* 39	16	Kathleen, *p.* 18
49	Jill, *p.* 35	67	Kay, *p.* 44
46	Jill, *p.* 33	27	Kayla, *p.* 24
51	Joanne, *p.* 36	15	Keane, *p.* 18
52	Jock, *p.* 36	35	Keenan, *p.* 28
50	Jock, *p.* 35	4	Keith, *p.* 12
61	Jody, *p.* 41	49	Kelly, *p.* 35
12	Joel, *p.* 16	48	Kelly, *p.* 34
52	John, *p.* 36	73	Kelvin, *p.* 47
52	Jonathon, *p.* 36	63	Kendall, *p.* 42
42	Jordan, *p.* 31	77	Kenneth, *p.* 49
17	Joscelyn, *p.* 19	8	Kent, *p.* 14
53	Joseph, *p.* 37	77	Kenton, *p.* 49
72	Joshua, *p.* 46	36	Kerry, *p.* 28
17	Joy, *p.* 19	33	Kerwin, *p.* 27
17	Joyce, *p.* 19	76	Kevin, *p.* 48

(For a complete list of 9000 names refer to _The Name Book_)

5	Kim, p. 13	34	Leila, p. 27
26	Kimball, p. 23	71	Lenora, p. 46
14	Kimberly, p. 17	45	Lenora, p. 33
12	Kingsley, p. 16	67	Leo, p. 44
12	Kingston, p. 16	54	Leo, p. 37
74	Kirkwood, p. 47	56	Leola, p. 38
75	Kirstin, p. 48	54	Leon, p. 37
73	Kit, p. 47	60	Leona, p. 40
20	Kit, p. 20	45	Leona, p. 33
16	Kitty, p. 18	54	Leonard, p. 37
40	Knut, p. 30	30	Leroy, p. 25
68	Kurt, p. 44	4	Lesley, p. 12
63	Kurt, p. 42	34	Leslie, p. 27
67	Kyle, p. 44	18	Lester, p. 19
76	Lacey, p. 48	25	Leta, p. 23
11	Lamar, p. 16	25	Letitia, p. 23
26	Lambert, p. 23	55	Levi, p. 38
68	Lamont, p. 44	55	Lewis, p. 38
78	Lana, p. 49	69	Leyland, p. 45
45	Lana, p. 33	34	Lila, p. 27
12	Lance, p. 16	17	Lila, p. 19
73	Langdon, p. 47	34	Lilac, p. 27
25	Larissa, p. 23	34	Lilian, p. 27
60	Laura, p. 40	34	Lily, p. 27
60	Laurel, p. 40	30	Lincoln, p. 25
73	Lauren, p. 47	79	Linda, p. 50
60	Lauren, p. 40	58	Linda, p. 39
1	Lavender, p. 11	2	Lindell, p. 11
75	Laverne, p. 48	24	Linden, p. 22
56	Lavetta, p. 38	8	Lindsey, p. 14
73	Lawrence, p. 47	78	Linette, p. 49
71	Leah, p. 46	54	Lionel, p. 37
71	Leana, p. 46	34	Lisa, p. 27
3	Leif, p. 12	7	Lisa, p. 14

(For a complete list of 9000 names refer to *The Name Book*)

10 Lloyd, *p.* 15	39 Mario, *p.* 30
33 Logan, *p.* 27	60 Marjorie, *p.* 40
38 Lola, *p.* 29	33 Mark, *p.* 27
3 Lombard, *p.* 12	62 Marlene, *p.* 41
9 Lona, *p.* 15	71 Marsha, *p.* 46
60 Loraine, *p.* 40	26 Marshall, *p.* 23
36 Lotus, *p.* 28	61 Martha, *p.* 41
55 Louis, *p.* 38	15 Martin, *p.* 18
56 Louise, *p.* 38	31 Martina, *p.* 26
15 Lowell, *p.* 18	61 Marty, *p.* 41
48 Loyal, *p.* 34	42 Marvin, *p.* 31
56 Luana, *p.* 38	62 Mary, *p.* 41
77 Lucas, *p.* 49	62 Maryanne, *p.* 41
57 Lucien, *p.* 39	10 Matthew, *p.* 15
71 Lucille, *p.* 46	51 Maude, *p.* 36
61 Lucrecia, *p.* 41	62 Maureen, *p.* 41
49 Luella, *p.* 35	41 Maureen, *p.* 31
56 Lulu, *p.* 38	63 Maurice, *p.* 42
25 Lydia, *p.* 23	49 Mavis, *p.* 35
24 Lyle, *p.* 22	57 Max, *p.* 39
49 Mabel, *p.* 35	57 Maximilian, *p.* 39
76 Mac, *p.* 48	5 Maxine, *p.* 13
58 Madeline, *p.* 39	57 Maxwell, *p.* 39
60 Madge, *p.* 40	68 Maynard, *p.* 44
3 Major, *p.* 12	5 Megan, *p.* 13
18 Malcolm, *p.* 19	14 Melanie, *p.* 17
14 Mandy, *p.* 17	78 Melba, *p.* 49
53 Manley, *p.* 37	14 Melinda, *p.* 17
4 Manville, *p.* 12	7 Melissa, *p.* 14
59 Marcel, *p.* 40	56 Melody, *p.* 38
71 Marcy, *p.* 46	67 Melvin, *p.* 44
60 Margaret, *p.* 40	56 Meredith, *p.* 38
60 Margo, *p.* 40	47 Meredith, *p.* 34
62 Marilyn, *p.* 41	40 Merle, *p.* 30

(For a complete list of 9000 names refer to *The Name Book*)

42	Mervin, *p.* 31	64	Napoleon, *p.* 42
38	Meryl, *p.* 29	79	Natalie, *p.* 50
64	Michael, *p.* 42	52	Nathanael, *p.* 36
41	Michele, *p.* 31	10	Neil, *p.* 15
64	Micky, *p.* 42	45	Nell, *p.* 33
79	Mildred, *p.* 50	39	Nelson, *p.* 30
4	Milford, *p.* 12	20	Nestor, *p.* 20
14	Millicent, *p.* 17	27	Neva, *p.* 24
74	Milton, *p.* 47	27	Nevada, *p.* 24
56	Missy, *p.* 38	13	Nevil, *p.* 17
64	Mitchell, *p.* 42	3	Nevin, *p.* 12
62	Molly, *p.* 41	6	Newall, *p.* 13
61	Mona, *p.* 41	18	Nicholas, *p.* 19
36	Mona, *p.* 28	41	Nicole, *p.* 31
61	Monica, *p.* 41	18	Nigel, *p.* 19
18	Monroe, *p.* 19	46	Nina, *p.* 33
37	Montague, *p.* 29	7	Nina, *p.* 14
67	Montgomery, *p.* 44	48	Noah, *p.* 34
37	Monty, *p.* 29	65	Noel, *p.* 43
62	Morgan, *p.* 41	38	Noel, *p.* 29
35	Morgan, *p.* 28	11	Nolan, *p.* 16
63	Morris, *p.* 42	45	Nora, *p.* 33
53	Mortimer, *p.* 37	3	Norbert, *p.* 12
74	Morton, *p.* 47	62	Norma, *p.* 41
13	Moses, *p.* 17	2	Norman, *p.* 11
22	Murdoch, *p.* 21	2	Norris, *p.* 11
62	Muriel, *p.* 41	20	Norton, *p.* 20
35	Murphy, *p.* 28	12	Octavius, *p.* 16
57	Murray, *p.* 39	53	Odell, *p.* 37
32	Myles, *p.* 26	56	Odella, *p.* 38
46	Nadine, *p.* 33	41	Olga, *p.* 31
11	Nairn, *p.* 16	3	Olin, *p.* 12
7	Nancy, *p.* 14	15	Oliver, *p.* 18
58	Naomi, *p.* 39	31	Olivia, *p.* 26

(For a complete list of 9000 names refer to *The Name Book*)

14 Opal, *p.* 17	1 Phyllis, *p.* 11
46 Oprah, *p.* 33	66 Pierce, *p.* 43
11 Orrick, *p.* 16	66 Pierre, *p.* 43
66 Orrin, *p.* 43	39 Prescott, *p.* 30
69 Orville, *p.* 45	67 Preston, *p.* 44
2 Osbert, *p.* 11	9 Prima, *p.* 15
8 Oscar, *p.* 14	7 Priscilla, *p.* 14
44 Osgood, *p.* 32	49 Pyrenia, *p.* 35
24 Osmond, *p.* 22	4 Quenby, *p.* 12
52 Otis, *p.* 36	20 Quentin, *p.* 20
73 Otto, *p.* 47	4 Quimby, *p.* 12
77 Owen, *p.* 49	68 Quincy, *p.* 44
65 Pablo, *p.* 43	71 Rachel, *p.* 46
49 Paige, *p.* 35	71 Rae, *p.* 46
25 Pamela, *p.* 23	66 Ralph, *p.* 43
27 Pansy, *p.* 24	44 Ralston, *p.* 32
22 Parker, *p.* 21	36 Ramona, *p.* 28
22 Pascal, *p.* 21	66 Randall, *p.* 43
5 Patience, *p.* 13	29 Raoul, *p.* 25
5 Patricia, *p.* 13	66 Raphael, *p.* 43
77 Patrick, *p.* 49	28 Raphaela, *p.* 24
5 Patsy, *p.* 13	68 Raymond, *p.* 44
65 Paul, *p.* 43	26 Reardon, *p.* 23
23 Paula, *p.* 22	5 Reba, *p.* 13
23 Pauline, *p.* 22	5 Rebecca, *p.* 13
60 Pearl, *p.* 40	18 Reed, *p.* 19
60 Peggy, *p.* 40	16 Regina, *p.* 18
75 Penny, *p.* 48	50 Reginald, *p.* 35
50 Percy, *p.* 35	18 Remington, *p.* 19
24 Perry, *p.* 22	61 Rene, *p.* 41
66 Peter, *p.* 43	51 Rene, *p.* 36
28 Phaidra, *p.* 24	61 Renee, *p.* 41
67 Philip, *p.* 44	53 Rexford, *p.* 37
75 Phoebe, *p.* 48	61 Rhea, *p.* 41

(For a complete list of 9000 names refer to *The Name Book*)

19	Rhonda, *p.* 20	69	Rupert, *p.* 45
22	Rice, *p.* 21	8	Russell, *p.* 14
64	Richard, *p.* 42	8	Rusty, *p.* 14
52	Richman, *p.* 36	62	Ruth, *p.* 41
24	Riley, *p.* 22	12	Rutherford, *p.* 16
60	Rita, *p.* 40	10	Ryan, *p.* 15
69	Robert, *p.* 45	79	Sabrina, *p.* 50
38	Roberta, *p.* 29	31	Salina, *p.* 26
69	Robin, *p.* 45	46	Sally, *p.* 33
72	Robinson, *p.* 46	38	Samantha, *p.* 29
18	Rochester, *p.* 19	33	Sampson, *p.* 27
73	Rodney, *p.* 47	53	Samuel, *p.* 37
55	Roger, *p.* 38	7	Sandra, *p.* 14
43	Romeo, *p.* 32	40	Sanford, *p.* 30
50	Ronald, *p.* 35	46	Sarah, *p.* 33
78	Rosalyn, *p.* 49	55	Sargent, *p.* 38
6	Roscoe, *p.* 13	18	Saul, *p.* 19
78	Rose, *p.* 49	31	Scarlett, *p.* 26
78	Rosemary, *p.* 49	76	Scott, *p.* 48
35	Ross, *p.* 28	52	Sean, *p.* 36
73	Rowan, *p.* 47	4	Seaton, *p.* 12
60	Rowena, *p.* 40	40	Sebastian, *p.* 30
7	Roxanne, *p.* 14	22	Sedgwick, *p.* 21
53	Roy, *p.* 37	79	Selena, *p.* 50
30	Roy, *p.* 25	4	Selig, *p.* 12
33	Royce, *p.* 27	62	Selma, *p.* 41
53	Rube, *p.* 37	23	Serena, *p.* 22
53	Ruben, *p.* 37	39	Seth, *p.* 30
11	Rudd, *p.* 16	3	Seward, *p.* 12
72	Rudolf, *p.* 46	55	Seymour, *p.* 38
15	Rudyard, *p.* 18	51	Shane, *p.* 36
57	Rufus, *p.* 39	17	Sharon, *p.* 19
2	Rufus, *p.* 11	17	Sheila, *p.* 19
22	Rugby, *p.* 21	35	Shelby, *p.* 28

(For a complete list of 9000 names refer to *The Name Book*)

(For a complete list of 9000 names refer to *The Name Book*)

9	Toni, *p.* 15	38	Velvet, *p.* 29
9	Tonia, *p.* 15	45	Venetia, *p.* 33
8	Tony, *p.* 14	65	Verner, *p.* 43
7	Tory, *p.* 14	22	Verner, *p.* 21
71	Tracey, *p.* 46	22	Vernon, *p.* 21
18	Tracey, *p.* 19	62	Veronica, *p.* 41
26	Travis, *p.* 23	19	Vicki, *p.* 20
69	Tremaine, *p.* 45	73	Victor, *p.* 47
68	Trevore, *p.* 44	19	Victoria, *p.* 20
57	Tripp, *p.* 39	74	Vincent, *p.* 47
62	Trixie, *p.* 41	23	Violet, *p.* 22
10	Troy, *p.* 15	40	Virgil, *p.* 30
61	Trudy, *p.* 41	75	Virginia, *p.* 48
69	Truman, *p.* 45	64	Vito, *p.* 42
6	Tucker, *p.* 13	38	Vivette, *p.* 29
77	Tyler, *p.* 49	38	Vivian, *p.* 29
68	Tyrone, *p.* 44	63	Vladimir, *p.* 42
77	Tyson, *p.* 49	55	Wadley, *p.* 38
49	Ulrica, *p.* 35	2	Waldo, *p.* 11
19	Ulrica, *p.* 20	69	Wallis, *p.* 45
44	Upton, *p.* 32	25	Wallis, *p.* 23
24	Uriel, *p.* 22	74	Walter, *p.* 47
61	Ursula, *p.* 41	16	Wanda, *p.* 18
63	, *p.* 42	39	Ward, *p.* 30
11	Vachel, *p.* 16	52	Warren, *p.* 36
52	Vail, *p.* 36	33	Washington, *p.* 27
67	Val, *p.* 44	67	Wayne, *p.* 44
20	Valentine, *p.* 20	47	Webster, *p.* 34
79	Valerie, *p.* 50	64	Welby, *p.* 42
66	Vance, *p.* 43	48	Wendell, *p.* 34
62	Vanessa, *p.* 41	16	Wendy, *p.* 18
62	Vanna, *p.* 41	7	Wendy, *p.* 14
28	Vashti, *p.* 24	70	Wesley, *p.* 45
52	Vaughan, *p.* 36	35	Whitcomb, *p.* 28

(For a complete list of 9000 names refer to *The Name Book*)

54 Wilbur, *p.* 37

40 Wilfred, *p.* 30

76 William, *p.* 48

43 Wilmur, *p.* 32

57 Winchell, *p.* 39

51 Winona, *p.* 36

18 Winthrop, *p.* 19

40 Wolfgang, *p.* 30

42 Woodrow, *p.* 31

74 Woody, *p.* 47

57 Worrell, *p.* 39

44 Wyatt, *p.* 32

20 Xavier, *p.* 20

65 Yale, *p.* 43

77 Yves, *p.* 49

78 Yvette, *p.* 49

79 Yvonne, *p.* 50

28 Zabrina, *p.* 24

40 Zacharias, *p.* 30

40 Zachary, *p.* 30

52 Zane, *p.* 36

52 Zebulon, *p.* 36

50 Zeke, *p.* 35

5 Zinia, *p.* 13

78 Zoe, *p.* 49

58 Zsa-Zsa, *p.* 39

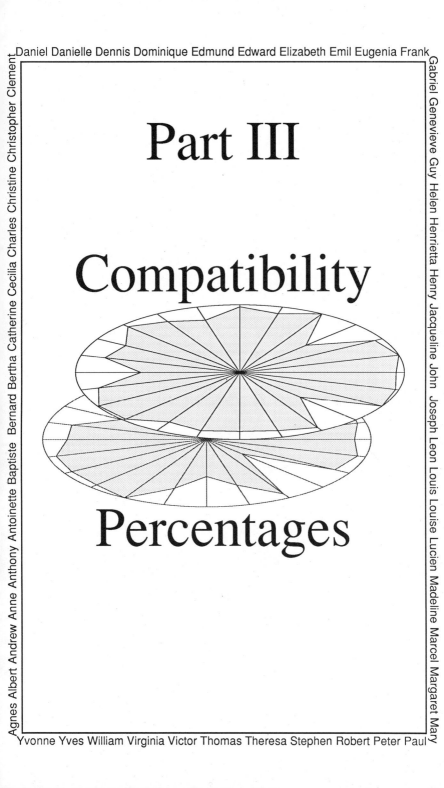

Part III

Compatibility

Percentages

1

How *Agnes* Relates To . . .

01 Agnes	85%	28 Denise	20%	55 Louis	95%
02 Albert	70%	29 Dennis	70%	56 Louise	10%
03 Alfred	75%	30 Dominic	90%	57 Lucien	50%
04 Alphonse	90%	31 Dominique	90%	58 Madeline	25%
05 Andrea	20%	32 Edmund	25%	59 Marcel	80%
06 Andrew	35%	33 Edward	95%	60 Margaret	45%
07 Anne	90%	34 Elizabeth	85%	61 Martha	60%
08 Anthony	60%	35 Emil	75%	62 Mary	90%
09 Antoinette	80%	36 Eugenia	90%	63 Maurice	30%
10 Baptiste	50%	37 Felix	50%	64 Michael	95%
11 Barnaby	65%	38 Frances	65%	65 Paul	15%
12 Bartholomew	85%	39 Frank	85%	66 Peter	95%
13 Bernard	75%	40 Gabriel	95%	67 Philip	90%
14 Bertha	85%	41 Genevieve	10%	68 Raymond	65%
15 Camille (M)	35%	42 George	55%	69 Robert	95%
16 Catherine	80%	43 Gerard	25%	70 Stephen	40%
17 Cecilia	60%	44 Guy	90%	71 Theresa	05%
18 Charles	25%	45 Helen	30%	72 Thomas	85%
19 Christine	15%	46 Henrietta	65%	73 Victor	35%
20 Christopher	80%	47 Henry	45%	74 Vincent	35%
21 Claire	95%	48 Hugh	40%	75 Virginia	35%
22 Claude	50%	49 Jacqueline	30%	76 William	50%
23 Claudia	55%	50 James	20%	77 Yves	45%
24 Clement	85%	51 Jeanne	40%	78 Yvette	15%
25 Colette	80%	52 John	40%	79 Yvonne	85%
26 Daniel	35%	53 Joseph	50%		
27 Danielle	45%	54 Leon	20%		

These are pilot names. See PART II: NAME DIRECTORY for your associated pilot name.

2

How *Albert* Relates To . . .

01 Agnes	85%	28 Denise	30%	55 Louis	40%
02 Albert	95%	29 Dennis	10%	56 Louise	50%
03 Alfred	35%	30 Dominic	75%	57 Lucien	75%
04 Alphonse	20%	31 Dominique	90%	58 Madeline	30%
05 Andrea	95%	32 Edmund	20%	59 Marcel	80%
06 Andrew	85%	33 Edward	10%	60 Margaret	90%
07 Anne	15%	34 Elizabeth	40%	61 Martha	30%
08 Anthony	60%	35 Emil	60%	62 Mary	80%
09 Antoinette	70%	36 Eugenia	20%	63 Maurice	80%
10 Baptiste	85%	37 Felix	80%	64 Michael	85%
11 Barnaby	10%	38 Frances	30%	65 Paul	40%
12 Bartholomew	50%	39 Frank	90%	66 Peter	50%
13 Bernard	80%	40 Gabriel	70%	67 Philip	80%
14 Bertha	25%	41 Genevieve	30%	68 Raymond	35%
15 Camille (M)	75%	42 George	80%	69 Robert	20%
16 Catherine	40%	43 Gerard	05%	70 Stephen	95%
17 Cecilia	55%	44 Guy	40%	71 Theresa	90%
18 Charles	90%	45 Helen	45%	72 Thomas	30%
19 Christine	05%	46 Henrietta	90%	73 Victor	25%
20 Christopher	30%	47 Henry	60%	74 Vincent	90%
21 Claire	80%	48 Hugh	25%	75 Virginia	85%
22 Claude	95%	49 Jacqueline	85%	76 William	50%
23 Claudia	50%	50 James	95%	77 Yves	35%
24 Clement	55%	51 Jeanne	45%	78 Yvette	95%
25 Colette	70%	52 John	65%	79 Yvonne	20%
26 Daniel	45%	53 Joseph	45%		
27 Danielle	60%	54 Leon	65%		

**These are pilot names. See PART II: NAME DIRECTORY
for your associated pilot name.**

3

How *Alfred* Relates To . . .

01 Agnes	70%	28 Denise	10%	55 Louis	45%
02 Albert	40%	29 Dennis	35%	56 Louise	45%
03 Alfred	55%	30 Dominic	90%	57 Lucien	95%
04 Alphonse	85%	31 Dominique	90%	58 Madeline	30%
05 Andrea	75%	32 Edmund	20%	59 Marcel	70%
06 Andrew	95%	33 Edward	80%	60 Margaret	40%
07 Anne	70%	34 Elizabeth	45%	61 Martha	20%
08 Anthony	40%	35 Emil	15%	62 Mary	80%
09 Antoinette	45%	36 Eugenia	15%	63 Maurice	15%
10 Baptiste	90%	37 Felix	35%	64 Michael	55%
11 Barnaby	30%	38 Frances	55%	65 Paul	60%
12 Bartholomew	70%	39 Frank	90%	66 Peter	85%
13 Bernard	95%	40 Gabriel	90%	67 Philip	30%
14 Bertha	20%	41 Genevieve	10%	68 Raymond	60%
15 Camille (M)	60%	42 George	85%	69 Robert	95%
16 Catherine	50%	43 Gerard	30%	70 Stephen	80%
17 Cecilia	45%	44 Guy	45%	71 Theresa	15%
18 Charles	90%	45 Helen	30%	72 Thomas	90%
19 Christine	80%	46 Henrietta	45%	73 Victor	95%
20 Christopher	30%	47 Henry	50%	74 Vincent	50%
21 Claire	60%	48 Hugh	50%	75 Virginia	10%
22 Claude	30%	49 Jacqueline	85%	76 William	95%
23 Claudia	50%	50 James	90%	77 Yves	45%
24 Clement	85%	51 Jeanne	55%	78 Yvette	35%
25 Colette	95%	52 John	40%	79 Yvonne	90%
26 Daniel	10%	53 Joseph	90%		
27 Danielle	25%	54 Leon	15%		

These are pilot names. See **PART II: NAME DIRECTORY** for your associated pilot name.

| 4 |

How *Alphonse* Relates To . . .

01 Agnes	70%		28 Denise	35%		55 Louis	30%
02 Albert	90%		29 Dennis	50%		56 Louise	25%
03 Alfred	55%		30 Dominic	50%		57 Lucien	90%
04 Alphonse	90%		31 Dominique	95%		58 Madeline	30%
05 Andrea	80%		32 Edmund	40%		59 Marcel	75%
06 Andrew	95%		33 Edward	95%		60 Margaret	30%
07 Anne	90%		34 Elizabeth	90%		61 Martha	65%
08 Anthony	40%		35 Emil	25%		62 Mary	60%
09 Antoinette	90%		36 Eugenia	40%		63 Maurice	10%
10 Baptiste	95%		37 Felix	50%		64 Michael	95%
11 Barnaby	40%		38 Frances	45%		65 Paul	85%
12 Bartholomew	90%		39 Frank	75%		66 Peter	60%
13 Bernard	45%		40 Gabriel	60%		67 Philip	85%
14 Bertha	35%		41 Genevieve	95%		68 Raymond	40%
15 Camille (M)	50%		42 George	05%		69 Robert	95%
16 Catherine	80%		43 Gerard	20%		70 Stephen	80%
17 Cecilia	30%		44 Guy	55%		71 Theresa	25%
18 Charles	95%		45 Helen	50%		72 Thomas	95%
19 Christine	20%		46 Henrietta	90%		73 Victor	10%
20 Christopher	50%		47 Henry	70%		74 Vincent	60%
21 Claire	80%		48 Hugh	95%		75 Virginia	85%
22 Claude	25%		49 Jacqueline	20%		76 William	85%
23 Claudia	35%		50 James	90%		77 Yves	20%
24 Clement	80%		51 Jeanne	50%		78 Yvette	30%
25 Colette	25%		52 John	95%		79 Yvonne	45%
26 Daniel	45%		53 Joseph	80%			
27 Danielle	20%		54 Leon	15%			

These are pilot names. See PART II: NAME DIRECTORY
for your associated pilot name.

5

How *Andrea* Relates To . . .

01 Agnes	90%	28 Denise	60%	55 Louis	50%
02 Albert	30%	29 Dennis	50%	56 Louise	40%
03 Alfred	95%	30 Dominic	85%	57 Lucien	85%
04 Alphonse	50%	31 Dominique	95%	58 Madeline	15%
05 Andrea	80%	32 Edmund	20%	59 Marcel	50%
06 Andrew	40%	33 Edward	10%	60 Margaret	90%
07 Anne	90%	34 Elizabeth	40%	61 Martha	50%
08 Anthony	45%	35 Emil	50%	62 Mary	95%
09 Antoinette	35%	36 Eugenia	95%	63 Maurice	55%
10 Baptiste	80%	37 Felix	45%	64 Michael	75%
11 Barnaby	60%	38 Frances	90%	65 Paul	45%
12 Bartholomew	95%	39 Frank	50%	66 Peter	95%
13 Bernard	30%	40 Gabriel	95%	67 Philip	30%
14 Bertha	85%	41 Genevieve	05%	68 Raymond	50%
15 Camille (M)	70%	42 George	20%	69 Robert	60%
16 Catherine	95%	43 Gerard	40%	70 Stephen	85%
17 Cecilia	90%	44 Guy	30%	71 Theresa	90%
18 Charles	95%	45 Helen	50%	72 Thomas	50%
19 Christine	80%	46 Henrietta	60%	73 Victor	10%
20 Christopher	95%	47 Henry	90%	74 Vincent	95%
21 Claire	90%	48 Hugh	50%	75 Virginia	70%
22 Claude	95%	49 Jacqueline	95%	76 William	50%
23 Claudia	80%	50 James	95%	77 Yves	50%
24 Clement	45%	51 Jeanne	50%	78 Yvette	15%
25 Colette	80%	52 John	85%	79 Yvonne	30%
26 Daniel	60%	53 Joseph	75%		
27 Danielle	25%	54 Leon	45%		

These are pilot names. See PART II: NAME DIRECTORY for your associated pilot name.

75

6

How *Andrew* Relates To . . .

01 Agnes	90%		28 Denise	45%		55 Louis	40%
02 Albert	60%		29 Dennis	20%		56 Louise	20%
03 Alfred	25%		30 Dominic	40%		57 Lucien	35%
04 Alphonse	30%		31 Dominique	80%		58 Madeline	20%
05 Andrea	90%		32 Edmund	45%		59 Marcel	55%
06 Andrew	65%		33 Edward	10%		60 Margaret	30%
07 Anne	95%		34 Elizabeth	35%		61 Martha	40%
08 Anthony	30%		35 Emil	45%		62 Mary	95%
09 Antoinette	55%		36 Eugenia	70%		63 Maurice	30%
10 Baptiste	45%		37 Felix	90%		64 Michael	95%
11 Barnaby	30%		38 Frances	30%		65 Paul	10%
12 Bartholomew	85%		39 Frank	85%		66 Peter	95%
13 Bernard	40%		40 Gabriel	25%		67 Philip	50%
14 Bertha	20%		41 Genevieve	45%		68 Raymond	80%
15 Camille (M)	40%		42 George	15%		69 Robert	95%
16 Catherine	25%		43 Gerard	85%		70 Stephen	20%
17 Cecilia	85%		44 Guy	30%		71 Theresa	35%
18 Charles	95%		45 Helen	90%		72 Thomas	45%
19 Christine	30%		46 Henrietta	45%		73 Victor	45%
20 Christopher	60%		47 Henry	35%		74 Vincent	10%
21 Claire	90%		48 Hugh	75%		75 Virginia	70%
22 Claude	35%		49 Jacqueline	95%		76 William	95%
23 Claudia	50%		50 James	95%		77 Yves	95%
24 Clement	70%		51 Jeanne	40%		78 Yvette	95%
25 Colette	55%		52 John	50%		79 Yvonne	20%
26 Daniel	65%		53 Joseph	85%			
27 Danielle	45%		54 Leon	30%			

These are pilot names. See **PART II: NAME DIRECTORY** for your associated pilot name.

7

How *Anne* Relates To . . .

01 Agnes	60%	28 Denise	70%	55 Louis	85%
02 Albert	90%	29 Dennis	30%	56 Louise	95%
03 Alfred	95%	30 Dominic	25%	57 Lucien	65%
04 Alphonse	50%	31 Dominique	60%	58 Madeline	25%
05 Andrea	80%	32 Edmund	40%	59 Marcel	70%
06 Andrew	95%	33 Edward	95%	60 Margaret	50%
07 Anne	40%	34 Elizabeth	30%	61 Martha	30%
08 Anthony	15%	35 Emil	50%	62 Mary	95%
09 Antoinette	30%	36 Eugenia	95%	63 Maurice	70%
10 Baptiste	55%	37 Felix	80%	64 Michael	95%
11 Barnaby	80%	38 Frances	85%	65 Paul	35%
12 Bartholomew	45%	39 Frank	50%	66 Peter	95%
13 Bernard	80%	40 Gabriel	95%	67 Philip	70%
14 Bertha	50%	41 Genevieve	50%	68 Raymond	50%
15 Camille (M)	50%	42 George	70%	69 Robert	60%
16 Catherine	85%	43 Gerard	35%	70 Stephen	90%
17 Cecilia	55%	44 Guy	65%	71 Theresa	45%
18 Charles	95%	45 Helen	90%	72 Thomas	85%
19 Christine	20%	46 Henrietta	50%	73 Victor	50%
20 Christopher	50%	47 Henry	25%	74 Vincent	35%
21 Claire	95%	48 Hugh	95%	75 Virginia	80%
22 Claude	25%	49 Jacqueline	45%	76 William	40%
23 Claudia	60%	50 James	70%	77 Yves	95%
24 Clement	45%	51 Jeanne	50%	78 Yvette	90%
25 Colette	90%	52 John	95%	79 Yvonne	50%
26 Daniel	80%	53 Joseph	60%		
27 Danielle	60%	54 Leon	65%		

These are pilot names. See PART II: NAME DIRECTORY for your associated pilot name.

8

How *Anthony* Relates To . . .

01 Agnes	80%		28 Denise	40%		55 Louis	70%
02 Albert	35%		29 Dennis	25%		56 Louise	55%
03 Alfred	95%		30 Dominic	80%		57 Lucien	85%
04 Alphonse	20%		31 Dominique	65%		58 Madeline	30%
05 Andrea	70%		32 Edmund	50%		59 Marcel	90%
06 Andrew	90%		33 Edward	95%		60 Margaret	50%
07 Anne	95%		34 Elizabeth	95%		61 Martha	95%
08 Anthony	95%		35 Emil	90%		62 Mary	85%
09 Antoinette	90%		36 Eugenia	30%		63 Maurice	10%
10 Baptiste	35%		37 Felix	95%		64 Michael	60%
11 Barnaby	60%		38 Frances	45%		65 Paul	50%
12 Bartholomew	50%		39 Frank	70%		66 Peter	95%
13 Bernard	90%		40 Gabriel	60%		67 Philip	90%
14 Bertha	10%		41 Genevieve	25%		68 Raymond	50%
15 Camille (M)	50%		42 George	80%		69 Robert	90%
16 Catherine	75%		43 Gerard	40%		70 Stephen	95%
17 Cecilia	45%		44 Guy	45%		71 Theresa	50%
18 Charles	95%		45 Helen	95%		72 Thomas	65%
19 Christine	40%		46 Henrietta	30%		73 Victor	80%
20 Christopher	50%		47 Henry	20%		74 Vincent	50%
21 Claire	85%		48 Hugh	80%		75 Virginia	95%
22 Claude	80%		49 Jacqueline	70%		76 William	95%
23 Claudia	55%		50 James	60%		77 Yves	45%
24 Clement	90%		51 Jeanne	30%		78 Yvette	55%
25 Colette	60%		52 John	90%		79 Yvonne	90%
26 Daniel	95%		53 Joseph	95%			
27 Danielle	60%		54 Leon	50%			

These are pilot names. See PART II: NAME DIRECTORY for your associated pilot name.

9

How *Antoinette* Relates To . . .

01	Agnes	80%	28	Denise	95%	55	Louis	80%
02	Albert	35%	29	Dennis	60%	56	Louise	70%
03	Alfred	90%	30	Dominic	30%	57	Lucien	60%
04	Alphonse	25%	31	Dominique	80%	58	Madeline	20%
05	Andrea	70%	32	Edmund	10%	59	Marcel	55%
06	Andrew	95%	33	Edward	95%	60	Margaret	35%
07	Anne	45%	34	Elizabeth	95%	61	Martha	10%
08	Anthony	35%	35	Emil	30%	62	Mary	80%
09	Antoinette	75%	36	Eugenia	20%	63	Maurice	50%
10	Baptiste	40%	37	Felix	60%	64	Michael	95%
11	Barnaby	60%	38	Frances	55%	65	Paul	20%
12	Bartholomew	95%	39	Frank	70%	66	Peter	75%
13	Bernard	15%	40	Gabriel	90%	67	Philip	50%
14	Bertha	60%	41	Genevieve	30%	68	Raymond	40%
15	Camille (M)	45%	42	George	95%	69	Robert	95%
16	Catherine	80%	43	Gerard	30%	70	Stephen	50%
17	Cecilia	45%	44	Guy	30%	71	Theresa	45%
18	Charles	50%	45	Helen	55%	72	Thomas	50%
19	Christine	10%	46	Henrietta	95%	73	Victor	15%
20	Christopher	85%	47	Henry	95%	74	Vincent	85%
21	Claire	50%	48	Hugh	45%	75	Virginia	95%
22	Claude	40%	49	Jacqueline	20%	76	William	95%
23	Claudia	50%	50	James	95%	77	Yves	95%
24	Clement	95%	51	Jeanne	45%	78	Yvette	20%
25	Colette	60%	52	John	60%	79	Yvonne	60%
26	Daniel	45%	53	Joseph	60%			
27	Danielle	80%	54	Leon	45%			

**These are pilot names. See PART II: NAME DIRECTORY
for your associated pilot name.**

10

How *Baptiste* Relates To . . .

01 Agnes	85%	28 Denise	60%	55 Louis	55%
02 Albert	45%	29 Dennis	30%	56 Louise	40%
03 Alfred	50%	30 Dominic	90%	57 Lucien	90%
04 Alphonse	95%	31 Dominique	50%	58 Madeline	80%
05 Andrea	95%	32 Edmund	20%	59 Marcel	95%
06 Andrew	60%	33 Edward	50%	60 Margaret	15%
07 Anne	80%	34 Elizabeth	95%	61 Martha	35%
08 Anthony	50%	35 Emil	60%	62 Mary	90%
09 Antoinette	70%	36 Eugenia	55%	63 Maurice	85%
10 Baptiste	45%	37 Felix	75%	64 Michael	95%
11 Barnaby	25%	38 Frances	95%	65 Paul	40%
12 Bartholomew	55%	39 Frank	80%	66 Peter	70%
13 Bernard	85%	40 Gabriel	80%	67 Philip	50%
14 Bertha	45%	41 Genevieve	15%	68 Raymond	95%
15 Camille (M)	50%	42 George	50%	69 Robert	60%
16 Catherine	95%	43 Gerard	45%	70 Stephen	40%
17 Cecilia	35%	44 Guy	50%	71 Theresa	50%
18 Charles	95%	45 Helen	30%	72 Thomas	80%
19 Christine	30%	46 Henrietta	60%	73 Victor	50%
20 Christopher	65%	47 Henry	95%	74 Vincent	15%
21 Claire	80%	48 Hugh	50%	75 Virginia	95%
22 Claude	85%	49 Jacqueline	90%	76 William	55%
23 Claudia	35%	50 James	95%	77 Yves	50%
24 Clement	50%	51 Jeanne	25%	78 Yvette	25%
25 Colette	95%	52 John	60%	79 Yvonne	80%
26 Daniel	10%	53 Joseph	95%		
27 Danielle	80%	54 Leon	95%		

**These are pilot names. See PART II: NAME DIRECTORY
for your associated pilot name.**

11

How *Barnaby* Relates To . . .

01 Agnes	25%	28 Denise	95%	55 Louis	70%
02 Albert	50%	29 Dennis	35%	56 Louise	50%
03 Alfred	85%	30 Dominic	10%	57 Lucien	95%
04 Alphonse	95%	31 Dominique	80%	58 Madeline	20%
05 Andrea	70%	32 Edmund	50%	59 Marcel	50%
06 Andrew	95%	33 Edward	95%	60 Margaret	35%
07 Anne	95%	34 Elizabeth	20%	61 Martha	20%
08 Anthony	10%	35 Emil	50%	62 Mary	60%
09 Antoinette	80%	36 Eugenia	45%	63 Maurice	50%
10 Baptiste	95%	37 Felix	50%	64 Michael	95%
11 Barnaby	80%	38 Frances	30%	65 Paul	25%
12 Bartholomew	30%	39 Frank	95%	66 Peter	50%
13 Bernard	50%	40 Gabriel	70%	67 Philip	85%
14 Bertha	80%	41 Genevieve	45%	68 Raymond	45%
15 Camille (M)	55%	42 George	50%	69 Robert	95%
16 Catherine	35%	43 Gerard	95%	70 Stephen	90%
17 Cecilia	95%	44 Guy	40%	71 Theresa	70%
18 Charles	80%	45 Helen	50%	72 Thomas	55%
19 Christine	45%	46 Henrietta	20%	73 Victor	50%
20 Christopher	50%	47 Henry	95%	74 Vincent	80%
21 Claire	95%	48 Hugh	50%	75 Virginia	45%
22 Claude	40%	49 Jacqueline	85%	76 William	55%
23 Claudia	95%	50 James	95%	77 Yves	50%
24 Clement	50%	51 Jeanne	95%	78 Yvette	95%
25 Colette	80%	52 John	25%	79 Yvonne	30%
26 Daniel	50%	53 Joseph	65%		
27 Danielle	70%	54 Leon	45%		

These are pilot names. See PART II: NAME DIRECTORY for your associated pilot name.

12

How *Bartholomew* Relates To . . .

01 Agnes	95%	28 Denise	65%	55 Louis	95%
02 Albert	20%	29 Dennis	90%	56 Louise	30%
03 Alfred	50%	30 Dominic	35%	57 Lucien	95%
04 Alphonse	60%	31 Dominique	60%	58 Madeline	50%
05 Andrea	80%	32 Edmund	45%	59 Marcel	95%
06 Andrew	95%	33 Edward	20%	60 Margaret	80%
07 Anne	95%	34 Elizabeth	55%	61 Martha	95%
08 Anthony	20%	35 Emil	50%	62 Mary	95%
09 Antoinette	30%	36 Eugenia	20%	63 Maurice	20%
10 Baptiste	95%	37 Felix	90%	64 Michael	70%
11 Barnaby	80%	38 Frances	95%	65 Paul	90%
12 Bartholomew	85%	39 Frank	15%	66 Peter	30%
13 Bernard	10%	40 Gabriel	65%	67 Philip	55%
14 Bertha	50%	41 Genevieve	30%	68 Raymond	80%
15 Camille (M)	90%	42 George	95%	69 Robert	95%
16 Catherine	80%	43 Gerard	60%	70 Stephen	95%
17 Cecilia	95%	44 Guy	50%	71 Theresa	45%
18 Charles	50%	45 Helen	95%	72 Thomas	95%
19 Christine	30%	46 Henrietta	10%	73 Victor	50%
20 Christopher	90%	47 Henry	95%	74 Vincent	90%
21 Claire	60%	48 Hugh	95%	75 Virginia	55%
22 Claude	50%	49 Jacqueline	05%	76 William	35%
23 Claudia	95%	50 James	50%	77 Yves	95%
24 Clement	95%	51 Jeanne	85%	78 Yvette	45%
25 Colette	80%	52 John	95%	79 Yvonne	50%
26 Daniel	30%	53 Joseph	95%		
27 Danielle	45%	54 Leon	50%		

**These are pilot names. See PART II: NAME DIRECTORY
for your associated pilot name.**

13

How *Bernard* Relates To . . .

01 Agnes	40%	28 Denise	95%	55 Louis	75%
02 Albert	60%	29 Dennis	50%	56 Louise	95%
03 Alfred	20%	30 Dominic	30%	57 Lucien	30%
04 Alphonse	50%	31 Dominique	95%	58 Madeline	95%
05 Andrea	75%	32 Edmund	95%	59 Marcel	95%
06 Andrew	95%	33 Edward	75%	60 Margaret	05%
07 Anne	50%	34 Elizabeth	30%	61 Martha	80%
08 Anthony	45%	35 Emil	85%	62 Mary	95%
09 Antoinette	50%	36 Eugenia	10%	63 Maurice	40%
10 Baptiste	80%	37 Felix	50%	64 Michael	95%
11 Barnaby	95%	38 Frances	50%	65 Paul	50%
12 Bartholomew	60%	39 Frank	95%	66 Peter	30%
13 Bernard	90%	40 Gabriel	80%	67 Philip	80%
14 Bertha	80%	41 Genevieve	95%	68 Raymond	50%
15 Camille (M)	50%	42 George	60%	69 Robert	95%
16 Catherine	10%	43 Gerard	50%	70 Stephen	95%
17 Cecilia	95%	44 Guy	95%	71 Theresa	95%
18 Charles	30%	45 Helen	45%	72 Thomas	70%
19 Christine	55%	46 Henrietta	25%	73 Victor	50%
20 Christopher	95%	47 Henry	95%	74 Vincent	20%
21 Claire	20%	48 Hugh	50%	75 Virginia	50%
22 Claude	80%	49 Jacqueline	95%	76 William	25%
23 Claudia	50%	50 James	95%	77 Yves	95%
24 Clement	45%	51 Jeanne	20%	78 Yvette	90%
25 Colette	95%	52 John	50%	79 Yvonne	45%
26 Daniel	30%	53 Joseph	95%		
27 Danielle	55%	54 Leon	45%		

These are pilot names. See **PART II: NAME DIRECTORY** for your associated pilot name.

14

How *Bertha* Relates To . . .

01	Agnes	50%	28	Denise	80%	55	Louis	85%
02	Albert	80%	29	Dennis	50%	56	Louise	15%
03	Alfred	50%	30	Dominic	95%	57	Lucien	50%
04	Alphonse	80%	31	Dominique	60%	58	Madeline	40%
05	Andrea	95%	32	Edmund	20%	59	Marcel	80%
06	Andrew	30%	33	Edward	30%	60	Margaret	15%
07	Anne	70%	34	Elizabeth	85%	61	Martha	95%
08	Anthony	95%	35	Emil	95%	62	Mary	95%
09	Antoinette	50%	36	Eugenia	50%	63	Maurice	25%
10	Baptiste	85%	37	Felix	90%	64	Michael	85%
11	Barnaby	80%	38	Frances	95%	65	Paul	65%
12	Bartholomew	30%	39	Frank	45%	66	Peter	50%
13	Bernard	10%	40	Gabriel	80%	67	Philip	95%
14	Bertha	30%	41	Genevieve	50%	68	Raymond	90%
15	Camille (M)	50%	42	George	55%	69	Robert	80%
16	Catherine	95%	43	Gerard	30%	70	Stephen	45%
17	Cecilia	60%	44	Guy	20%	71	Theresa	55%
18	Charles	20%	45	Helen	30%	72	Thomas	95%
19	Christine	45%	46	Henrietta	60%	73	Victor	05%
20	Christopher	90%	47	Henry	45%	74	Vincent	05%
21	Claire	95%	48	Hugh	95%	75	Virginia	95%
22	Claude	70%	49	Jacqueline	20%	76	William	95%
23	Claudia	15%	50	James	75%	77	Yves	65%
24	Clement	50%	51	Jeanne	25%	78	Yvette	50%
25	Colette	90%	52	John	50%	79	Yvonne	15%
26	Daniel	70%	53	Joseph	80%			
27	Danielle	30%	54	Leon	95%			

**These are pilot names. See PART II: NAME DIRECTORY
for your associated pilot name.**

15

How *Camille (M)* Relates To . . .

01	Agnes	80%	28	Denise	50%	55	Louis	80%
02	Albert	95%	29	Dennis	45%	56	Louise	45%
03	Alfred	60%	30	Dominic	95%	57	Lucien	95%
04	Alphonse	50%	31	Dominique	95%	58	Madeline	25%
05	Andrea	85%	32	Edmund	40%	59	Marcel	95%
06	Andrew	95%	33	Edward	10%	60	Margaret	85%
07	Anne	95%	34	Elizabeth	85%	61	Martha	95%
08	Anthony	70%	35	Emil	50%	62	Mary	80%
09	Antoinette	20%	36	Eugenia	45%	63	Maurice	60%
10	Baptiste	50%	37	Felix	50%	64	Michael	55%
11	Barnaby	50%	38	Frances	25%	65	Paul	30%
12	Bartholomew	95%	39	Frank	90%	66	Peter	95%
13	Bernard	60%	40	Gabriel	95%	67	Philip	70%
14	Bertha	30%	41	Genevieve	35%	68	Raymond	95%
15	Camille (M)	55%	42	George	95%	69	Robert	50%
16	Catherine	10%	43	Gerard	50%	70	Stephen	90%
17	Cecilia	50%	44	Guy	20%	71	Theresa	90%
18	Charles	95%	45	Helen	85%	72	Thomas	95%
19	Christine	15%	46	Henrietta	90%	73	Victor	45%
20	Christopher	50%	47	Henry	95%	74	Vincent	90%
21	Claire	60%	48	Hugh	60%	75	Virginia	95%
22	Claude	75%	49	Jacqueline	50%	76	William	95%
23	Claudia	95%	50	James	50%	77	Yves	65%
24	Clement	80%	51	Jeanne	65%	78	Yvette	95%
25	Colette	55%	52	John	90%	79	Yvonne	60%
26	Daniel	25%	53	Joseph	80%			
27	Danielle	60%	54	Leon	55%			

**These are pilot names. See PART II: NAME DIRECTORY
for your associated pilot name.**

16

How *Catherine* Relates To . . .

01 Agnes	20%	28 Denise	50%	55 Louis	45%
02 Albert	90%	29 Dennis	15%	56 Louise	20%
03 Alfred	50%	30 Dominic	10%	57 Lucien	40%
04 Alphonse	60%	31 Dominique	95%	58 Madeline	20%
05 Andrea	80%	32 Edmund	45%	59 Marcel	80%
06 Andrew	90%	33 Edward	95%	60 Margaret	30%
07 Anne	25%	34 Elizabeth	45%	61 Martha	95%
08 Anthony	70%	35 Emil	15%	62 Mary	90%
09 Antoinette	40%	36 Eugenia	30%	63 Maurice	35%
10 Baptiste	85%	37 Felix	45%	64 Michael	95%
11 Barnaby	40%	38 Frances	15%	65 Paul	45%
12 Bartholomew	95%	39 Frank	95%	66 Peter	80%
13 Bernard	20%	40 Gabriel	85%	67 Philip	50%
14 Bertha	95%	41 Genevieve	95%	68 Raymond	45%
15 Camille (M)	45%	42 George	95%	69 Robert	95%
16 Catherine	85%	43 Gerard	10%	70 Stephen	85%
17 Cecilia	55%	44 Guy	45%	71 Theresa	15%
18 Charles	95%	45 Helen	20%	72 Thomas	90%
19 Christine	05%	46 Henrietta	45%	73 Victor	95%
20 Christopher	90%	47 Henry	80%	74 Vincent	25%
21 Claire	95%	48 Hugh	50%	75 Virginia	95%
22 Claude	90%	49 Jacqueline	95%	76 William	95%
23 Claudia	30%	50 James	90%	77 Yves	95%
24 Clement	95%	51 Jeanne	30%	78 Yvette	45%
25 Colette	40%	52 John	95%	79 Yvonne	95%
26 Daniel	95%	53 Joseph	95%		
27 Danielle	35%	54 Leon	05%		

**These are pilot names. See PART II: NAME DIRECTORY
for your associated pilot name.**

$$\boxed{17}$$

How *Cecilia* Relates To . . .

01 Agnes	35%	28 Denise	95%	55 Louis	50%
02 Albert	85%	29 Dennis	50%	56 Louise	45%
03 Alfred	50%	30 Dominic	20%	57 Lucien	95%
04 Alphonse	20%	31 Dominique	95%	58 Madeline	45%
05 Andrea	60%	32 Edmund	25%	59 Marcel	95%
06 Andrew	95%	33 Edward	45%	60 Margaret	30%
07 Anne	50%	34 Elizabeth	95%	61 Martha	50%
08 Anthony	65%	35 Emil	55%	62 Mary	65%
09 Antoinette	45%	36 Eugenia	40%	63 Maurice	50%
10 Baptiste	55%	37 Felix	50%	64 Michael	90%
11 Barnaby	85%	38 Frances	95%	65 Paul	95%
12 Bartholomew	80%	39 Frank	95%	66 Peter	60%
13 Bernard	20%	40 Gabriel	60%	67 Philip	10%
14 Bertha	50%	41 Genevieve	50%	68 Raymond	50%
15 Camille (M)	70%	42 George	95%	69 Robert	70%
16 Catherine	50%	43 Gerard	40%	70 Stephen	95%
17 Cecilia	40%	44 Guy	40%	71 Theresa	90%
18 Charles	30%	45 Helen	95%	72 Thomas	95%
19 Christine	55%	46 Henrietta	90%	73 Victor	20%
20 Christopher	95%	47 Henry	55%	74 Vincent	05%
21 Claire	95%	48 Hugh	20%	75 Virginia	95%
22 Claude	40%	49 Jacqueline	50%	76 William	95%
23 Claudia	70%	50 James	60%	77 Yves	30%
24 Clement	95%	51 Jeanne	20%	78 Yvette	95%
25 Colette	95%	52 John	95%	79 Yvonne	30%
26 Daniel	35%	53 Joseph	50%		
27 Danielle	15%	54 Leon	10%		

**These are pilot names. See PART II: NAME DIRECTORY
for your associated pilot name.**

18

How *Charles* Relates To . . .

01 Agnes	80%	28 Denise	90%	55 Louis	55%
02 Albert	95%	29 Dennis	20%	56 Louise	20%
03 Alfred	20%	30 Dominic	95%	57 Lucien	55%
04 Alphonse	50%	31 Dominique	90%	58 Madeline	10%
05 Andrea	85%	32 Edmund	40%	59 Marcel	95%
06 Andrew	95%	33 Edward	95%	60 Margaret	45%
07 Anne	95%	34 Elizabeth	60%	61 Martha	55%
08 Anthony	45%	35 Emil	20%	62 Mary	95%
09 Antoinette	85%	36 Eugenia	10%	63 Maurice	05%
10 Baptiste	30%	37 Felix	35%	64 Michael	95%
11 Barnaby	50%	38 Frances	85%	65 Paul	95%
12 Bartholomew	95%	39 Frank	10%	66 Peter	85%
13 Bernard	80%	40 Gabriel	95%	67 Philip	20%
14 Bertha	25%	41 Genevieve	15%	68 Raymond	45%
15 Camille (M)	55%	42 George	60%	69 Robert	95%
16 Catherine	95%	43 Gerard	45%	70 Stephen	95%
17 Cecilia	30%	44 Guy	10%	71 Theresa	05%
18 Charles	95%	45 Helen	20%	72 Thomas	50%
19 Christine	45%	46 Henrietta	80%	73 Victor	10%
20 Christopher	60%	47 Henry	30%	74 Vincent	20%
21 Claire	95%	48 Hugh	50%	75 Virginia	50%
22 Claude	25%	49 Jacqueline	25%	76 William	95%
23 Claudia	15%	50 James	95%	77 Yves	95%
24 Clement	50%	51 Jeanne	35%	78 Yvette	90%
25 Colette	95%	52 John	95%	79 Yvonne	95%
26 Daniel	15%	53 Joseph	85%		
27 Danielle	50%	54 Leon	30%		

**These are pilot names. See PART II: NAME DIRECTORY
for your associated pilot name.**

19

How *Christine* Relates To . . .

01 Agnes	30%	28 Denise	85%	55 Louis	90%
02 Albert	60%	29 Dennis	50%	56 Louise	40%
03 Alfred	50%	30 Dominic	45%	57 Lucien	50%
04 Alphonse	40%	31 Dominique	20%	58 Madeline	60%
05 Andrea	80%	32 Edmund	80%	59 Marcel	80%
06 Andrew	95%	33 Edward	95%	60 Margaret	30%
07 Anne	95%	34 Elizabeth	30%	61 Martha	95%
08 Anthony	45%	35 Emil	45%	62 Mary	90%
09 Antoinette	25%	36 Eugenia	45%	63 Maurice	20%
10 Baptiste	95%	37 Felix	40%	64 Michael	80%
11 Barnaby	60%	38 Frances	95%	65 Paul	70%
12 Bartholomew	80%	39 Frank	50%	66 Peter	95%
13 Bernard	35%	40 Gabriel	80%	67 Philip	50%
14 Bertha	85%	41 Genevieve	05%	68 Raymond	60%
15 Camille (M)	50%	42 George	90%	69 Robert	90%
16 Catherine	10%	43 Gerard	95%	70 Stephen	80%
17 Cecilia	90%	44 Guy	90%	71 Theresa	60%
18 Charles	70%	45 Helen	95%	72 Thomas	95%
19 Christine	25%	46 Henrietta	90%	73 Victor	50%
20 Christopher	55%	47 Henry	30%	74 Vincent	95%
21 Claire	90%	48 Hugh	95%	75 Virginia	45%
22 Claude	95%	49 Jacqueline	15%	76 William	50%
23 Claudia	45%	50 James	95%	77 Yves	95%
24 Clement	50%	51 Jeanne	80%	78 Yvette	95%
25 Colette	95%	52 John	45%	79 Yvonne	90%
26 Daniel	25%	53 Joseph	95%		
27 Danielle	10%	54 Leon	20%		

These are pilot names. See **PART II: NAME DIRECTORY** for your associated pilot name.

20

How *Christopher* Relates To . . .

01 Agnes	80%		28 Denise	25%		55 Louis	85%
02 Albert	60%		29 Dennis	95%		56 Louise	95%
03 Alfred	50%		30 Dominic	95%		57 Lucien	65%
04 Alphonse	95%		31 Dominique	40%		58 Madeline	20%
05 Andrea	80%		32 Edmund	85%		59 Marcel	95%
06 Andrew	35%		33 Edward	50%		60 Margaret	25%
07 Anne	95%		34 Elizabeth	80%		61 Martha	80%
08 Anthony	50%		35 Emil	55%		62 Mary	95%
09 Antoinette	40%		36 Eugenia	25%		63 Maurice	95%
10 Baptiste	95%		37 Felix	80%		64 Michael	75%
11 Barnaby	45%		38 Frances	95%		65 Paul	50%
12 Bartholomew	50%		39 Frank	50%		66 Peter	90%
13 Bernard	95%		40 Gabriel	80%		67 Philip	75%
14 Bertha	50%		41 Genevieve	10%		68 Raymond	60%
15 Camille (M)	80%		42 George	95%		69 Robert	95%
16 Catherine	95%		43 Gerard	40%		70 Stephen	95%
17 Cecilia	90%		44 Guy	95%		71 Theresa	95%
18 Charles	95%		45 Helen	15%		72 Thomas	60%
19 Christine	50%		46 Henrietta	85%		73 Victor	40%
20 Christopher	85%		47 Henry	50%		74 Vincent	50%
21 Claire	95%		48 Hugh	30%		75 Virginia	95%
22 Claude	20%		49 Jacqueline	45%		76 William	80%
23 Claudia	95%		50 James	95%		77 Yves	95%
24 Clement	50%		51 Jeanne	45%		78 Yvette	60%
25 Colette	95%		52 John	95%		79 Yvonne	95%
26 Daniel	95%		53 Joseph	95%			
27 Danielle	80%		54 Leon	50%			

These are pilot names. See PART II: NAME DIRECTORY for your associated pilot name.

21

How *Claire* Relates To . . .

01 Agnes	90%	28 Denise	90%	55 Louis	30%
02 Albert	50%	29 Dennis	55%	56 Louise	05%
03 Alfred	35%	30 Dominic	45%	57 Lucien	75%
04 Alphonse	50%	31 Dominique	20%	58 Madeline	30%
05 Andrea	95%	32 Edmund	95%	59 Marcel	95%
06 Andrew	95%	33 Edward	40%	60 Margaret	50%
07 Anne	95%	34 Elizabeth	70%	61 Martha	20%
08 Anthony	20%	35 Emil	50%	62 Mary	95%
09 Antoinette	50%	36 Eugenia	30%	63 Maurice	10%
10 Baptiste	80%	37 Felix	50%	64 Michael	60%
11 Barnaby	95%	38 Frances	40%	65 Paul	50%
12 Bartholomew	20%	39 Frank	95%	66 Peter	35%
13 Bernard	50%	40 Gabriel	80%	67 Philip	95%
14 Bertha	10%	41 Genevieve	20%	68 Raymond	80%
15 Camille (M)	95%	42 George	95%	69 Robert	85%
16 Catherine	85%	43 Gerard	40%	70 Stephen	35%
17 Cecilia	35%	44 Guy	95%	71 Theresa	25%
18 Charles	65%	45 Helen	95%	72 Thomas	95%
19 Christine	95%	46 Henrietta	40%	73 Victor	95%
20 Christopher	50%	47 Henry	80%	74 Vincent	70%
21 Claire	45%	48 Hugh	50%	75 Virginia	20%
22 Claude	90%	49 Jacqueline	95%	76 William	50%
23 Claudia	45%	50 James	15%	77 Yves	95%
24 Clement	50%	51 Jeanne	95%	78 Yvette	10%
25 Colette	90%	52 John	95%	79 Yvonne	50%
26 Daniel	40%	53 Joseph	20%		
27 Danielle	60%	54 Leon	95%		

**These are pilot names. See PART II: NAME DIRECTORY
for your associated pilot name.**

22

How *Claude* Relates To . . .

01	Agnes	90%	28	Denise	50%	55	Louis	95%
02	Albert	95%	29	Dennis	40%	56	Louise	45%
03	Alfred	70%	30	Dominic	95%	57	Lucien	70%
04	Alphonse	25%	31	Dominique	65%	58	Madeline	40%
05	Andrea	95%	32	Edmund	50%	59	Marcel	90%
06	Andrew	60%	33	Edward	35%	60	Margaret	45%
07	Anne	45%	34	Elizabeth	95%	61	Martha	45%
08	Anthony	50%	35	Emil	45%	62	Mary	90%
09	Antoinette	90%	36	Eugenia	35%	63	Maurice	50%
10	Baptiste	60%	37	Felix	95%	64	Michael	85%
11	Barnaby	95%	38	Frances	30%	65	Paul	55%
12	Bartholomew	15%	39	Frank	80%	66	Peter	40%
13	Bernard	75%	40	Gabriel	95%	67	Philip	95%
14	Bertha	95%	41	Genevieve	45%	68	Raymond	95%
15	Camille (M)	50%	42	George	60%	69	Robert	40%
16	Catherine	80%	43	Gerard	15%	70	Stephen	80%
17	Cecilia	40%	44	Guy	95%	71	Theresa	10%
18	Charles	95%	45	Helen	95%	72	Thomas	95%
19	Christine	10%	46	Henrietta	60%	73	Victor	20%
20	Christopher	55%	47	Henry	45%	74	Vincent	90%
21	Claire	60%	48	Hugh	90%	75	Virginia	60%
22	Claude	95%	49	Jacqueline	95%	76	William	50%
23	Claudia	20%	50	James	65%	77	Yves	95%
24	Clement	95%	51	Jeanne	90%	78	Yvette	30%
25	Colette	65%	52	John	95%	79	Yvonne	50%
26	Daniel	40%	53	Joseph	60%			
27	Danielle	95%	54	Leon	40%			

These are pilot names. See PART II: NAME DIRECTORY for your associated pilot name.

| 23 |

How *Claudia* Relates To . . .

01 Agnes	90%		28 Denise	60%		55 Louis	45%
02 Albert	95%		29 Dennis	10%		56 Louise	15%
03 Alfred	20%		30 Dominic	95%		57 Lucien	80%
04 Alphonse	50%		31 Dominique	45%		58 Madeline	15%
05 Andrea	10%		32 Edmund	25%		59 Marcel	45%
06 Andrew	95%		33 Edward	85%		60 Margaret	95%
07 Anne	95%		34 Elizabeth	05%		61 Martha	45%
08 Anthony	05%		35 Emil	50%		62 Mary	35%
09 Antoinette	60%		36 Eugenia	50%		63 Maurice	10%
10 Baptiste	85%		37 Felix	90%		64 Michael	50%
11 Barnaby	50%		38 Frances	95%		65 Paul	05%
12 Bartholomew	80%		39 Frank	45%		66 Peter	85%
13 Bernard	50%		40 Gabriel	45%		67 Philip	95%
14 Bertha	95%		41 Genevieve	20%		68 Raymond	25%
15 Camille (M)	60%		42 George	95%		69 Robert	95%
16 Catherine	20%		43 Gerard	35%		70 Stephen	90%
17 Cecilia	95%		44 Guy	10%		71 Theresa	45%
18 Charles	10%		45 Helen	50%		72 Thomas	95%
19 Christine	60%		46 Henrietta	95%		73 Victor	45%
20 Christopher	80%		47 Henry	50%		74 Vincent	10%
21 Claire	95%		48 Hugh	45%		75 Virginia	50%
22 Claude	40%		49 Jacqueline	80%		76 William	95%
23 Claudia	75%		50 James	70%		77 Yves	95%
24 Clement	80%		51 Jeanne	95%		78 Yvette	90%
25 Colette	95%		52 John	50%		79 Yvonne	50%
26 Daniel	50%		53 Joseph	60%			
27 Danielle	25%		54 Leon	50%			

These are pilot names. See PART II: NAME DIRECTORY for your associated pilot name.

24

How *Clement* Relates To . . .

01 Agnes	95%	28 Denise	90%	55 Louis	80%
02 Albert	80%	29 Dennis	60%	56 Louise	95%
03 Alfred	65%	30 Dominic	95%	57 Lucien	70%
04 Alphonse	95%	31 Dominique	80%	58 Madeline	50%
05 Andrea	50%	32 Edmund	30%	59 Marcel	95%
06 Andrew	60%	33 Edward	50%	60 Margaret	95%
07 Anne	95%	34 Elizabeth	95%	61 Martha	95%
08 Anthony	75%	35 Emil	85%	62 Mary	90%
09 Antoinette	30%	36 Eugenia	95%	63 Maurice	30%
10 Baptiste	95%	37 Felix	60%	64 Michael	80%
11 Barnaby	65%	38 Frances	65%	65 Paul	95%
12 Bartholomew	95%	39 Frank	95%	66 Peter	95%
13 Bernard	20%	40 Gabriel	95%	67 Philip	60%
14 Bertha	50%	41 Genevieve	40%	68 Raymond	45%
15 Camille (M)	95%	42 George	60%	69 Robert	95%
16 Catherine	05%	43 Gerard	50%	70 Stephen	60%
17 Cecilia	95%	44 Guy	30%	71 Theresa	60%
18 Charles	80%	45 Helen	60%	72 Thomas	70%
19 Christine	40%	46 Henrietta	95%	73 Victor	95%
20 Christopher	95%	47 Henry	95%	74 Vincent	95%
21 Claire	80%	48 Hugh	90%	75 Virginia	35%
22 Claude	50%	49 Jacqueline	15%	76 William	95%
23 Claudia	95%	50 James	95%	77 Yves	95%
24 Clement	90%	51 Jeanne	45%	78 Yvette	45%
25 Colette	60%	52 John	80%	79 Yvonne	50%
26 Daniel	95%	53 Joseph	95%		
27 Danielle	45%	54 Leon	50%		

**These are pilot names. See PART II: NAME DIRECTORY
for your associated pilot name.**

25

How *Colette* Relates To . . .

01 Agnes	95%	28 Denise	30%	55 Louis	55%
02 Albert	70%	29 Dennis	70%	56 Louise	40%
03 Alfred	45%	30 Dominic	60%	57 Lucien	85%
04 Alphonse	50%	31 Dominique	45%	58 Madeline	25%
05 Andrea	75%	32 Edmund	80%	59 Marcel	95%
06 Andrew	95%	33 Edward	10%	60 Margaret	95%
07 Anne	40%	34 Elizabeth	25%	61 Martha	40%
08 Anthony	30%	35 Emil	85%	62 Mary	95%
09 Antoinette	10%	36 Eugenia	30%	63 Maurice	25%
10 Baptiste	90%	37 Felix	85%	64 Michael	95%
11 Barnaby	60%	38 Frances	45%	65 Paul	20%
12 Bartholomew	95%	39 Frank	45%	66 Peter	95%
13 Bernard	20%	40 Gabriel	80%	67 Philip	95%
14 Bertha	95%	41 Genevieve	95%	68 Raymond	20%
15 Camille (M)	30%	42 George	70%	69 Robert	95%
16 Catherine	50%	43 Gerard	35%	70 Stephen	95%
17 Cecilia	80%	44 Guy	30%	71 Theresa	10%
18 Charles	95%	45 Helen	50%	72 Thomas	95%
19 Christine	05%	46 Henrietta	40%	73 Victor	25%
20 Christopher	60%	47 Henry	80%	74 Vincent	05%
21 Claire	95%	48 Hugh	60%	75 Virginia	50%
22 Claude	20%	49 Jacqueline	40%	76 William	95%
23 Claudia	25%	50 James	70%	77 Yves	95%
24 Clement	50%	51 Jeanne	60%	78 Yvette	20%
25 Colette	70%	52 John	90%	79 Yvonne	95%
26 Daniel	55%	53 Joseph	95%		
27 Danielle	15%	54 Leon	45%		

These are pilot names. See PART II: NAME DIRECTORY for your associated pilot name.

26

How *Daniel* Relates To . . .

01 Agnes	15%		28 Denise	55%		55 Louis	80%
02 Albert	80%		29 Dennis	95%		56 Louise	55%
03 Alfred	95%		30 Dominic	30%		57 Lucien	95%
04 Alphonse	60%		31 Dominique	95%		58 Madeline	25%
05 Andrea	95%		32 Edmund	60%		59 Marcel	95%
06 Andrew	95%		33 Edward	45%		60 Margaret	70%
07 Anne	20%		34 Elizabeth	95%		61 Martha	95%
08 Anthony	80%		35 Emil	65%		62 Mary	60%
09 Antoinette	50%		36 Eugenia	45%		63 Maurice	95%
10 Baptiste	95%		37 Felix	95%		64 Michael	40%
11 Barnaby	45%		38 Frances	60%		65 Paul	85%
12 Bartholomew	80%		39 Frank	20%		66 Peter	85%
13 Bernard	60%		40 Gabriel	80%		67 Philip	35%
14 Bertha	50%		41 Genevieve	20%		68 Raymond	90%
15 Camille (M)	90%		42 George	50%		69 Robert	95%
16 Catherine	35%		43 Gerard	30%		70 Stephen	90%
17 Cecilia	50%		44 Guy	45%		71 Theresa	10%
18 Charles	95%		45 Helen	85%		72 Thomas	50%
19 Christine	85%		46 Henrietta	45%		73 Victor	85%
20 Christopher	45%		47 Henry	95%		74 Vincent	95%
21 Claire	60%		48 Hugh	20%		75 Virginia	95%
22 Claude	50%		49 Jacqueline	80%		76 William	95%
23 Claudia	45%		50 James	90%		77 Yves	30%
24 Clement	95%		51 Jeanne	95%		78 Yvette	95%
25 Colette	20%		52 John	55%		79 Yvonne	45%
26 Daniel	60%		53 Joseph	50%			
27 Danielle	30%		54 Leon	30%			

**These are pilot names. See PART II: NAME DIRECTORY
for your associated pilot name.**

27

How *Danielle* Relates To . . .

01	Agnes	10%	28	Denise	95%	55	Louis	85%
02	Albert	80%	29	Dennis	40%	56	Louise	50%
03	Alfred	50%	30	Dominic	60%	57	Lucien	65%
04	Alphonse	95%	31	Dominique	95%	58	Madeline	45%
05	Andrea	70%	32	Edmund	25%	59	Marcel	50%
06	Andrew	95%	33	Edward	95%	60	Margaret	95%
07	Anne	50%	34	Elizabeth	10%	61	Martha	50%
08	Anthony	95%	35	Emil	95%	62	Mary	80%
09	Antoinette	20%	36	Eugenia	50%	63	Maurice	85%
10	Baptiste	95%	37	Felix	95%	64	Michael	95%
11	Barnaby	40%	38	Frances	60%	65	Paul	35%
12	Bartholomew	50%	39	Frank	10%	66	Peter	95%
13	Bernard	75%	40	Gabriel	95%	67	Philip	95%
14	Bertha	10%	41	Genevieve	05%	68	Raymond	95%
15	Camille (M)	95%	42	George	70%	69	Robert	50%
16	Catherine	20%	43	Gerard	35%	70	Stephen	30%
17	Cecilia	85%	44	Guy	45%	71	Theresa	95%
18	Charles	95%	45	Helen	95%	72	Thomas	55%
19	Christine	05%	46	Henrietta	20%	73	Victor	95%
20	Christopher	50%	47	Henry	95%	74	Vincent	95%
21	Claire	90%	48	Hugh	50%	75	Virginia	30%
22	Claude	60%	49	Jacqueline	95%	76	William	95%
23	Claudia	45%	50	James	95%	77	Yves	50%
24	Clement	85%	51	Jeanne	45%	78	Yvette	10%
25	Colette	95%	52	John	30%	79	Yvonne	95%
26	Daniel	65%	53	Joseph	95%			
27	Danielle	50%	54	Leon	60%			

These are pilot names. See PART II: NAME DIRECTORY for your associated pilot name.

28

How *Denise* Relates To . . .

01	Agnes	40%	28	Denise	20%	55	Louis	90%
02	Albert	60%	29	Dennis	15%	56	Louise	30%
03	Alfred	50%	30	Dominic	05%	57	Lucien	60%
04	Alphonse	70%	31	Dominique	50%	58	Madeline	15%
05	Andrea	80%	32	Edmund	95%	59	Marcel	50%
06	Andrew	30%	33	Edward	50%	60	Margaret	95%
07	Anne	50%	34	Elizabeth	05%	61	Martha	10%
08	Anthony	95%	35	Emil	60%	62	Mary	85%
09	Antoinette	50%	36	Eugenia	50%	63	Maurice	50%
10	Baptiste	60%	37	Felix	10%	64	Michael	80%
11	Barnaby	20%	38	Frances	25%	65	Paul	45%
12	Bartholomew	50%	39	Frank	50%	66	Peter	95%
13	Bernard	10%	40	Gabriel	80%	67	Philip	95%
14	Bertha	05%	41	Genevieve	05%	68	Raymond	10%
15	Camille (M)	60%	42	George	50%	69	Robert	80%
16	Catherine	85%	43	Gerard	15%	70	Stephen	95%
17	Cecilia	95%	44	Guy	35%	71	Theresa	10%
18	Charles	95%	45	Helen	60%	72	Thomas	50%
19	Christine	10%	46	Henrietta	55%	73	Victor	85%
20	Christopher	50%	47	Henry	95%	74	Vincent	05%
21	Claire	90%	48	Hugh	15%	75	Virginia	15%
22	Claude	60%	49	Jacqueline	50%	76	William	50%
23	Claudia	95%	50	James	60%	77	Yves	95%
24	Clement	95%	51	Jeanne	95%	78	Yvette	50%
25	Colette	55%	52	John	50%	79	Yvonne	05%
26	Daniel	50%	53	Joseph	95%			
27	Danielle	30%	54	Leon	20%			

These are pilot names. See PART II: NAME DIRECTORY for your associated pilot name.

29

How *Dennis* Relates To . . .

01	Agnes	80%	28	Denise	45%	55	Louis	65%
02	Albert	95%	29	Dennis	80%	56	Louise	80%
03	Alfred	85%	30	Dominic	85%	57	Lucien	30%
04	Alphonse	60%	31	Dominique	95%	58	Madeline	45%
05	Andrea	95%	32	Edmund	50%	59	Marcel	85%
06	Andrew	30%	33	Edward	95%	60	Margaret	95%
07	Anne	90%	34	Elizabeth	35%	61	Martha	55%
08	Anthony	95%	35	Emil	50%	62	Mary	95%
09	Antoinette	45%	36	Eugenia	95%	63	Maurice	25%
10	Baptiste	80%	37	Felix	60%	64	Michael	85%
11	Barnaby	65%	38	Frances	80%	65	Paul	95%
12	Bartholomew	45%	39	Frank	45%	66	Peter	85%
13	Bernard	85%	40	Gabriel	90%	67	Philip	50%
14	Bertha	30%	41	Genevieve	10%	68	Raymond	60%
15	Camille (M)	95%	42	George	95%	69	Robert	95%
16	Catherine	40%	43	Gerard	55%	70	Stephen	90%
17	Cecilia	95%	44	Guy	45%	71	Theresa	30%
18	Charles	90%	45	Helen	50%	72	Thomas	40%
19	Christine	45%	46	Henrietta	30%	73	Victor	95%
20	Christopher	85%	47	Henry	85%	74	Vincent	30%
21	Claire	60%	48	Hugh	95%	75	Virginia	80%
22	Claude	95%	49	Jacqueline	95%	76	William	95%
23	Claudia	40%	50	James	60%	77	Yves	95%
24	Clement	65%	51	Jeanne	80%	78	Yvette	25%
25	Colette	85%	52	John	50%	79	Yvonne	95%
26	Daniel	60%	53	Joseph	95%			
27	Danielle	95%	54	Leon	95%			

These are pilot names. See PART II: NAME DIRECTORY for your associated pilot name.

30

How *Dominic* Relates To . . .

01 Agnes	90%	28 Denise	95%	55 Louis	90%
02 Albert	50%	29 Dennis	50%	56 Louise	35%
03 Alfred	70%	30 Dominic	95%	57 Lucien	95%
04 Alphonse	85%	31 Dominique	30%	58 Madeline	20%
05 Andrea	90%	32 Edmund	60%	59 Marcel	80%
06 Andrew	95%	33 Edward	50%	60 Margaret	50%
07 Anne	95%	34 Elizabeth	80%	61 Martha	45%
08 Anthony	20%	35 Emil	95%	62 Mary	95%
09 Antoinette	40%	36 Eugenia	65%	63 Maurice	75%
10 Baptiste	95%	37 Felix	95%	64 Michael	95%
11 Barnaby	25%	38 Frances	85%	65 Paul	35%
12 Bartholomew	90%	39 Frank	50%	66 Peter	95%
13 Bernard	95%	40 Gabriel	95%	67 Philip	80%
14 Bertha	60%	41 Genevieve	45%	68 Raymond	50%
15 Camille (M)	95%	42 George	90%	69 Robert	85%
16 Catherine	35%	43 Gerard	45%	70 Stephen	35%
17 Cecilia	50%	44 Guy	40%	71 Theresa	45%
18 Charles	95%	45 Helen	90%	72 Thomas	85%
19 Christine	55%	46 Henrietta	60%	73 Victor	45%
20 Christopher	80%	47 Henry	50%	74 Vincent	20%
21 Claire	95%	48 Hugh	45%	75 Virginia	90%
22 Claude	50%	49 Jacqueline	95%	76 William	85%
23 Claudia	95%	50 James	80%	77 Yves	40%
24 Clement	85%	51 Jeanne	20%	78 Yvette	95%
25 Colette	95%	52 John	95%	79 Yvonne	20%
26 Daniel	45%	53 Joseph	95%		
27 Danielle	85%	54 Leon	35%		

**These are pilot names. See PART II: NAME DIRECTORY
for your associated pilot name.**

31

How *Dominique* Relates To . . .

01 Agnes	65%	28 Denise	45%	55 Louis	65%
02 Albert	80%	29 Dennis	80%	56 Louise	95%
03 Alfred	50%	30 Dominic	95%	57 Lucien	95%
04 Alphonse	95%	31 Dominique	45%	58 Madeline	70%
05 Andrea	80%	32 Edmund	45%	59 Marcel	50%
06 Andrew	25%	33 Edward	95%	60 Margaret	90%
07 Anne	95%	34 Elizabeth	20%	61 Martha	60%
08 Anthony	65%	35 Emil	95%	62 Mary	95%
09 Antoinette	15%	36 Eugenia	95%	63 Maurice	50%
10 Baptiste	80%	37 Felix	10%	64 Michael	25%
11 Barnaby	45%	38 Frances	45%	65 Paul	95%
12 Bartholomew	60%	39 Frank	95%	66 Peter	95%
13 Bernard	50%	40 Gabriel	55%	67 Philip	45%
14 Bertha	95%	41 Genevieve	10%	68 Raymond	20%
15 Camille (M)	30%	42 George	60%	69 Robert	50%
16 Catherine	95%	43 Gerard	90%	70 Stephen	25%
17 Cecilia	50%	44 Guy	95%	71 Theresa	95%
18 Charles	80%	45 Helen	15%	72 Thomas	90%
19 Christine	95%	46 Henrietta	60%	73 Victor	20%
20 Christopher	45%	47 Henry	45%	74 Vincent	45%
21 Claire	55%	48 Hugh	95%	75 Virginia	80%
22 Claude	20%	49 Jacqueline	15%	76 William	95%
23 Claudia	60%	50 James	50%	77 Yves	95%
24 Clement	50%	51 Jeanne	35%	78 Yvette	10%
25 Colette	90%	52 John	95%	79 Yvonne	95%
26 Daniel	95%	53 Joseph	80%		
27 Danielle	30%	54 Leon	50%		

These are pilot names. See PART II: NAME DIRECTORY for your associated pilot name.

32

How *Edmund* Relates To . . .

01 Agnes	50%	28 Denise	50%	55 Louis	45%
02 Albert	80%	29 Dennis	30%	56 Louise	95%
03 Alfred	95%	30 Dominic	95%	57 Lucien	50%
04 Alphonse	95%	31 Dominique	40%	58 Madeline	85%
05 Andrea	50%	32 Edmund	75%	59 Marcel	95%
06 Andrew	60%	33 Edward	10%	60 Margaret	35%
07 Anne	95%	34 Elizabeth	95%	61 Martha	45%
08 Anthony	95%	35 Emil	70%	62 Mary	95%
09 Antoinette	20%	36 Eugenia	30%	63 Maurice	50%
10 Baptiste	60%	37 Felix	95%	64 Michael	95%
11 Barnaby	45%	38 Frances	95%	65 Paul	45%
12 Bartholomew	95%	39 Frank	25%	66 Peter	95%
13 Bernard	40%	40 Gabriel	35%	67 Philip	95%
14 Bertha	10%	41 Genevieve	05%	68 Raymond	40%
15 Camille (M)	45%	42 George	95%	69 Robert	95%
16 Catherine	20%	43 Gerard	10%	70 Stephen	25%
17 Cecilia	95%	44 Guy	45%	71 Theresa	30%
18 Charles	30%	45 Helen	10%	72 Thomas	50%
19 Christine	25%	46 Henrietta	45%	73 Victor	65%
20 Christopher	50%	47 Henry	50%	74 Vincent	45%
21 Claire	80%	48 Hugh	90%	75 Virginia	95%
22 Claude	35%	49 Jacqueline	30%	76 William	95%
23 Claudia	95%	50 James	50%	77 Yves	95%
24 Clement	10%	51 Jeanne	10%	78 Yvette	45%
25 Colette	80%	52 John	55%	79 Yvonne	80%
26 Daniel	50%	53 Joseph	95%		
27 Danielle	05%	54 Leon	60%		

**These are pilot names. See PART II: NAME DIRECTORY
for your associated pilot name.**

33

How *Edward* Relates To . . .

01 Agnes	30%		28 Denise	10%		55 Louis	90%
02 Albert	80%		29 Dennis	95%		56 Louise	45%
03 Alfred	20%		30 Dominic	60%		57 Lucien	85%
04 Alphonse	75%		31 Dominique	85%		58 Madeline	10%
05 Andrea	30%		32 Edmund	50%		59 Marcel	95%
06 Andrew	95%		33 Edward	35%		60 Margaret	45%
07 Anne	95%		34 Elizabeth	85%		61 Martha	50%
08 Anthony	45%		35 Emil	95%		62 Mary	85%
09 Antoinette	50%		36 Eugenia	20%		63 Maurice	20%
10 Baptiste	95%		37 Felix	55%		64 Michael	50%
11 Barnaby	20%		38 Frances	80%		65 Paul	85%
12 Bartholomew	85%		39 Frank	50%		66 Peter	60%
13 Bernard	50%		40 Gabriel	95%		67 Philip	95%
14 Bertha	10%		41 Genevieve	45%		68 Raymond	30%
15 Camille (M)	85%		42 George	95%		69 Robert	95%
16 Catherine	40%		43 Gerard	40%		70 Stephen	85%
17 Cecilia	95%		44 Guy	45%		71 Theresa	65%
18 Charles	25%		45 Helen	95%		72 Thomas	95%
19 Christine	50%		46 Henrietta	45%		73 Victor	35%
20 Christopher	90%		47 Henry	65%		74 Vincent	05%
21 Claire	95%		48 Hugh	50%		75 Virginia	80%
22 Claude	55%		49 Jacqueline	80%		76 William	50%
23 Claudia	35%		50 James	40%		77 Yves	85%
24 Clement	95%		51 Jeanne	50%		78 Yvette	40%
25 Colette	95%		52 John	90%		79 Yvonne	95%
26 Daniel	10%		53 Joseph	95%			
27 Danielle	50%		54 Leon	40%			

These are pilot names. See **PART II: NAME DIRECTORY**
for your associated pilot name.

34

How *Elizabeth* Relates To . . .

01 Agnes	90%		28 Denise	60%		55 Louis	50%
02 Albert	20%		29 Dennis	35%		56 Louise	70%
03 Alfred	60%		30 Dominic	45%		57 Lucien	45%
04 Alphonse	45%		31 Dominique	20%		58 Madeline	15%
05 Andrea	50%		32 Edmund	95%		59 Marcel	45%
06 Andrew	50%		33 Edward	20%		60 Margaret	90%
07 Anne	25%		34 Elizabeth	40%		61 Martha	70%
08 Anthony	85%		35 Emil	90%		62 Mary	95%
09 Antoinette	95%		36 Eugenia	05%		63 Maurice	50%
10 Baptiste	80%		37 Felix	50%		64 Michael	95%
11 Barnaby	20%		38 Frances	60%		65 Paul	15%
12 Bartholomew	40%		39 Frank	80%		66 Peter	90%
13 Bernard	50%		40 Gabriel	80%		67 Philip	60%
14 Bertha	95%		41 Genevieve	25%		68 Raymond	50%
15 Camille (M)	70%		42 George	85%		69 Robert	20%
16 Catherine	10%		43 Gerard	45%		70 Stephen	95%
17 Cecilia	50%		44 Guy	35%		71 Theresa	65%
18 Charles	95%		45 Helen	50%		72 Thomas	50%
19 Christine	15%		46 Henrietta	20%		73 Victor	15%
20 Christopher	90%		47 Henry	95%		74 Vincent	95%
21 Claire	55%		48 Hugh	50%		75 Virginia	80%
22 Claude	25%		49 Jacqueline	30%		76 William	90%
23 Claudia	50%		50 James	60%		77 Yves	50%
24 Clement	45%		51 Jeanne	35%		78 Yvette	80%
25 Colette	95%		52 John	95%		79 Yvonne	95%
26 Daniel	15%		53 Joseph	80%			
27 Danielle	95%		54 Leon	10%			

These are pilot names. See PART II: NAME DIRECTORY for your associated pilot name.

35

How *Emil* Relates To . . .

01	Agnes	70%	28	Denise	50%	55	Louis	50%
02	Albert	40%	29	Dennis	30%	56	Louise	95%
03	Alfred	95%	30	Dominic	10%	57	Lucien	95%
04	Alphonse	60%	31	Dominique	90%	58	Madeline	95%
05	Andrea	45%	32	Edmund	45%	59	Marcel	45%
06	Andrew	80%	33	Edward	95%	60	Margaret	25%
07	Anne	20%	34	Elizabeth	80%	61	Martha	45%
08	Anthony	70%	35	Emil	85%	62	Mary	95%
09	Antoinette	10%	36	Eugenia	85%	63	Maurice	85%
10	Baptiste	95%	37	Felix	50%	64	Michael	95%
11	Barnaby	30%	38	Frances	25%	65	Paul	10%
12	Bartholomew	95%	39	Frank	15%	66	Peter	95%
13	Bernard	45%	40	Gabriel	90%	67	Philip	55%
14	Bertha	50%	41	Genevieve	10%	68	Raymond	95%
15	Camille (M)	95%	42	George	65%	69	Robert	45%
16	Catherine	95%	43	Gerard	95%	70	Stephen	40%
17	Cecilia	60%	44	Guy	95%	71	Theresa	40%
18	Charles	90%	45	Helen	20%	72	Thomas	70%
19	Christine	40%	46	Henrietta	30%	73	Victor	95%
20	Christopher	95%	47	Henry	95%	74	Vincent	90%
21	Claire	50%	48	Hugh	95%	75	Virginia	95%
22	Claude	95%	49	Jacqueline	55%	76	William	85%
23	Claudia	45%	50	James	95%	77	Yves	50%
24	Clement	80%	51	Jeanne	95%	78	Yvette	45%
25	Colette	95%	52	John	90%	79	Yvonne	60%
26	Daniel	20%	53	Joseph	95%			
27	Danielle	95%	54	Leon	20%			

These are pilot names. See **PART II: NAME DIRECTORY**
for your associated pilot name.

36

How *Eugenia* Relates To . . .

01	Agnes	80%	28	Denise	30%	55	Louis	50%
02	Albert	20%	29	Dennis	60%	56	Louise	20%
03	Alfred	40%	30	Dominic	80%	57	Lucien	65%
04	Alphonse	50%	31	Dominique	45%	58	Madeline	90%
05	Andrea	70%	32	Edmund	30%	59	Marcel	95%
06	Andrew	85%	33	Edward	05%	60	Margaret	45%
07	Anne	05%	34	Elizabeth	35%	61	Martha	05%
08	Anthony	95%	35	Emil	05%	62	Mary	95%
09	Antoinette	10%	36	Eugenia	35%	63	Maurice	50%
10	Baptiste	50%	37	Felix	45%	64	Michael	95%
11	Barnaby	50%	38	Frances	80%	65	Paul	95%
12	Bartholomew	60%	39	Frank	95%	66	Peter	95%
13	Bernard	95%	40	Gabriel	55%	67	Philip	50%
14	Bertha	05%	41	Genevieve	30%	68	Raymond	90%
15	Camille (M)	80%	42	George	95%	69	Robert	95%
16	Catherine	15%	43	Gerard	20%	70	Stephen	95%
17	Cecilia	60%	44	Guy	95%	71	Theresa	45%
18	Charles	80%	45	Helen	40%	72	Thomas	95%
19	Christine	50%	46	Henrietta	30%	73	Victor	05%
20	Christopher	30%	47	Henry	50%	74	Vincent	20%
21	Claire	95%	48	Hugh	95%	75	Virginia	90%
22	Claude	95%	49	Jacqueline	90%	76	William	80%
23	Claudia	20%	50	James	95%	77	Yves	95%
24	Clement	95%	51	Jeanne	50%	78	Yvette	40%
25	Colette	65%	52	John	30%	79	Yvonne	95%
26	Daniel	50%	53	Joseph	85%			
27	Danielle	10%	54	Leon	10%			

**These are pilot names. See PART II: NAME DIRECTORY
for your associated pilot name.**

37

How *Felix* Relates To . . .

01 Agnes	95%	28 Denise	35%	55 Louis	30%
02 Albert	95%	29 Dennis	80%	56 Louise	95%
03 Alfred	95%	30 Dominic	60%	57 Lucien	45%
04 Alphonse	30%	31 Dominique	95%	58 Madeline	50%
05 Andrea	85%	32 Edmund	30%	59 Marcel	95%
06 Andrew	95%	33 Edward	95%	60 Margaret	45%
07 Anne	95%	34 Elizabeth	20%	61 Martha	20%
08 Anthony	95%	35 Emil	95%	62 Mary	95%
09 Antoinette	60%	36 Eugenia	45%	63 Maurice	80%
10 Baptiste	80%	37 Felix	95%	64 Michael	95%
11 Barnaby	95%	38 Frances	40%	65 Paul	60%
12 Bartholomew	95%	39 Frank	50%	66 Peter	95%
13 Bernard	30%	40 Gabriel	95%	67 Philip	95%
14 Bertha	45%	41 Genevieve	10%	68 Raymond	95%
15 Camille (M)	85%	42 George	55%	69 Robert	95%
16 Catherine	60%	43 Gerard	30%	70 Stephen	85%
17 Cecilia	50%	44 Guy	60%	71 Theresa	90%
18 Charles	95%	45 Helen	85%	72 Thomas	95%
19 Christine	55%	46 Henrietta	50%	73 Victor	40%
20 Christopher	95%	47 Henry	45%	74 Vincent	95%
21 Claire	90%	48 Hugh	85%	75 Virginia	65%
22 Claude	95%	49 Jacqueline	95%	76 William	95%
23 Claudia	80%	50 James	90%	77 Yves	95%
24 Clement	95%	51 Jeanne	60%	78 Yvette	40%
25 Colette	95%	52 John	35%	79 Yvonne	05%
26 Daniel	80%	53 Joseph	95%		
27 Danielle	35%	54 Leon	95%		

**These are pilot names. See PART II: NAME DIRECTORY
for your associated pilot name.**

38

How *Frances* Relates To . . .

01	Agnes	85%	28	Denise	90%	55	Louis	60%
02	Albert	50%	29	Dennis	60%	56	Louise	50%
03	Alfred	30%	30	Dominic	95%	57	Lucien	90%
04	Alphonse	95%	31	Dominique	10%	58	Madeline	95%
05	Andrea	90%	32	Edmund	95%	59	Marcel	85%
06	Andrew	95%	33	Edward	80%	60	Margaret	65%
07	Anne	60%	34	Elizabeth	75%	61	Martha	95%
08	Anthony	30%	35	Emil	35%	62	Mary	95%
09	Antoinette	80%	36	Eugenia	50%	63	Maurice	25%
10	Baptiste	95%	37	Felix	45%	64	Michael	80%
11	Barnaby	65%	38	Frances	40%	65	Paul	95%
12	Bartholomew	90%	39	Frank	85%	66	Peter	65%
13	Bernard	40%	40	Gabriel	55%	67	Philip	25%
14	Bertha	50%	41	Genevieve	05%	68	Raymond	95%
15	Camille (M)	85%	42	George	80%	69	Robert	50%
16	Catherine	20%	43	Gerard	55%	70	Stephen	80%
17	Cecilia	50%	44	Guy	65%	71	Theresa	95%
18	Charles	95%	45	Helen	30%	72	Thomas	80%
19	Christine	80%	46	Henrietta	60%	73	Victor	45%
20	Christopher	95%	47	Henry	90%	74	Vincent	95%
21	Claire	95%	48	Hugh	95%	75	Virginia	60%
22	Claude	50%	49	Jacqueline	25%	76	William	95%
23	Claudia	80%	50	James	95%	77	Yves	30%
24	Clement	55%	51	Jeanne	55%	78	Yvette	95%
25	Colette	90%	52	John	80%	79	Yvonne	65%
26	Daniel	40%	53	Joseph	95%			
27	Danielle	50%	54	Leon	50%			

**These are pilot names. See PART II: NAME DIRECTORY
for your associated pilot name.**

COMPATIBILITY PERCENTAGES

39

How *Frank* Relates To . . .

01 Agnes	80%		28 Denise	70%		55 Louis	90%
02 Albert	50%		29 Dennis	50%		56 Louise	70%
03 Alfred	70%		30 Dominic	95%		57 Lucien	85%
04 Alphonse	35%		31 Dominique	95%		58 Madeline	25%
05 Andrea	80%		32 Edmund	45%		59 Marcel	95%
06 Andrew	95%		33 Edward	55%		60 Margaret	10%
07 Anne	60%		34 Elizabeth	90%		61 Martha	45%
08 Anthony	50%		35 Emil	45%		62 Mary	85%
09 Antoinette	55%		36 Eugenia	80%		63 Maurice	20%
10 Baptiste	25%		37 Felix	30%		64 Michael	95%
11 Barnaby	50%		38 Frances	35%		65 Paul	80%
12 Bartholomew	85%		39 Frank	55%		66 Peter	70%
13 Bernard	95%		40 Gabriel	50%		67 Philip	95%
14 Bertha	20%		41 Genevieve	30%		68 Raymond	95%
15 Camille (M)	50%		42 George	95%		69 Robert	35%
16 Catherine	95%		43 Gerard	35%		70 Stephen	50%
17 Cecilia	10%		44 Guy	40%		71 Theresa	15%
18 Charles	65%		45 Helen	80%		72 Thomas	95%
19 Christine	15%		46 Henrietta	55%		73 Victor	45%
20 Christopher	30%		47 Henry	20%		74 Vincent	85%
21 Claire	50%		48 Hugh	50%		75 Virginia	40%
22 Claude	95%		49 Jacqueline	95%		76 William	75%
23 Claudia	70%		50 James	95%		77 Yves	95%
24 Clement	90%		51 Jeanne	50%		78 Yvette	30%
25 Colette	65%		52 John	60%		79 Yvonne	40%
26 Daniel	95%		53 Joseph	95%			
27 Danielle	70%		54 Leon	30%			

These are pilot names. See **PART II: NAME DIRECTORY** for your associated pilot name.

40

How *Gabriel* Relates To . . .

01 Agnes	80%	28 Denise	85%	55 Louis	80%
02 Albert	50%	29 Dennis	95%	56 Louise	45%
03 Alfred	60%	30 Dominic	95%	57 Lucien	60%
04 Alphonse	95%	31 Dominique	35%	58 Madeline	50%
05 Andrea	80%	32 Edmund	95%	59 Marcel	95%
06 Andrew	95%	33 Edward	60%	60 Margaret	20%
07 Anne	30%	34 Elizabeth	80%	61 Martha	30%
08 Anthony	95%	35 Emil	45%	62 Mary	95%
09 Antoinette	80%	36 Eugenia	20%	63 Maurice	50%
10 Baptiste	95%	37 Felix	80%	64 Michael	95%
11 Barnaby	45%	38 Frances	10%	65 Paul	40%
12 Bartholomew	95%	39 Frank	50%	66 Peter	95%
13 Bernard	90%	40 Gabriel	80%	67 Philip	60%
14 Bertha	95%	41 Genevieve	20%	68 Raymond	45%
15 Camille (M)	35%	42 George	70%	69 Robert	95%
16 Catherine	95%	43 Gerard	95%	70 Stephen	95%
17 Cecilia	80%	44 Guy	95%	71 Theresa	90%
18 Charles	85%	45 Helen	95%	72 Thomas	95%
19 Christine	95%	46 Henrietta	35%	73 Victor	30%
20 Christopher	60%	47 Henry	95%	74 Vincent	05%
21 Claire	35%	48 Hugh	60%	75 Virginia	80%
22 Claude	95%	49 Jacqueline	45%	76 William	65%
23 Claudia	55%	50 James	95%	77 Yves	95%
24 Clement	95%	51 Jeanne	10%	78 Yvette	90%
25 Colette	95%	52 John	60%	79 Yvonne	60%
26 Daniel	50%	53 Joseph	95%		
27 Danielle	25%	54 Leon	45%		

These are pilot names. See PART II: NAME DIRECTORY for your associated pilot name.

41

How *Genevieve* Relates To . . .

01 Agnes	10%	28 Denise	45%	55 Louis	50%
02 Albert	50%	29 Dennis	10%	56 Louise	95%
03 Alfred	15%	30 Dominic	50%	57 Lucien	15%
04 Alphonse	30%	31 Dominique	95%	58 Madeline	95%
05 Andrea	80%	32 Edmund	60%	59 Marcel	50%
06 Andrew	60%	33 Edward	95%	60 Margaret	30%
07 Anne	95%	34 Elizabeth	95%	61 Martha	95%
08 Anthony	80%	35 Emil	80%	62 Mary	85%
09 Antoinette	95%	36 Eugenia	95%	63 Maurice	10%
10 Baptiste	80%	37 Felix	15%	64 Michael	95%
11 Barnaby	30%	38 Frances	85%	65 Paul	55%
12 Bartholomew	50%	39 Frank	95%	66 Peter	70%
13 Bernard	95%	40 Gabriel	95%	67 Philip	95%
14 Bertha	95%	41 Genevieve	25%	68 Raymond	25%
15 Camille (M)	30%	42 George	15%	69 Robert	70%
16 Catherine	60%	43 Gerard	10%	70 Stephen	35%
17 Cecilia	45%	44 Guy	30%	71 Theresa	95%
18 Charles	85%	45 Helen	50%	72 Thomas	40%
19 Christine	95%	46 Henrietta	50%	73 Victor	70%
20 Christopher	80%	47 Henry	80%	74 Vincent	95%
21 Claire	95%	48 Hugh	15%	75 Virginia	45%
22 Claude	20%	49 Jacqueline	95%	76 William	95%
23 Claudia	55%	50 James	95%	77 Yves	55%
24 Clement	95%	51 Jeanne	95%	78 Yvette	10%
25 Colette	65%	52 John	40%	79 Yvonne	95%
26 Daniel	95%	53 Joseph	65%		
27 Danielle	95%	54 Leon	20%		

These are pilot names. See **PART II: NAME DIRECTORY** for your associated pilot name.

42

How *George* Relates To . . .

01	Agnes	90%	28	Denise	20%	55	Louis	70%
02	Albert	70%	29	Dennis	30%	56	Louise	30%
03	Alfred	50%	30	Dominic	35%	57	Lucien	40%
04	Alphonse	60%	31	Dominique	70%	58	Madeline	10%
05	Andrea	70%	32	Edmund	80%	59	Marcel	85%
06	Andrew	90%	33	Edward	95%	60	Margaret	15%
07	Anne	30%	34	Elizabeth	80%	61	Martha	20%
08	Anthony	35%	35	Emil	05%	62	Mary	95%
09	Antoinette	40%	36	Eugenia	90%	63	Maurice	40%
10	Baptiste	85%	37	Felix	20%	64	Michael	45%
11	Barnaby	50%	38	Frances	90%	65	Paul	20%
12	Bartholomew	80%	39	Frank	50%	66	Peter	80%
13	Bernard	95%	40	Gabriel	95%	67	Philip	50%
14	Bertha	20%	41	Genevieve	20%	68	Raymond	35%
15	Camille (M)	45%	42	George	50%	69	Robert	85%
16	Catherine	85%	43	Gerard	30%	70	Stephen	85%
17	Cecilia	35%	44	Guy	70%	71	Theresa	35%
18	Charles	95%	45	Helen	40%	72	Thomas	45%
19	Christine	20%	46	Henrietta	50%	73	Victor	80%
20	Christopher	35%	47	Henry	90%	74	Vincent	10%
21	Claire	90%	48	Hugh	85%	75	Virginia	85%
22	Claude	95%	49	Jacqueline	25%	76	William	50%
23	Claudia	40%	50	James	10%	77	Yves	40%
24	Clement	30%	51	Jeanne	55%	78	Yvette	90%
25	Colette	40%	52	John	45%	79	Yvonne	25%
26	Daniel	25%	53	Joseph	95%			
27	Danielle	45%	54	Leon	15%			

**These are pilot names. See PART II: NAME DIRECTORY
for your associated pilot name.**

43

How *Gerard* Relates To . . .

01	Agnes	20%	28	Denise	30%	55	Louis	90%
02	Albert	45%	29	Dennis	10%	56	Louise	55%
03	Alfred	60%	30	Dominic	95%	57	Lucien	50%
04	Alphonse	50%	31	Dominique	30%	58	Madeline	80%
05	Andrea	95%	32	Edmund	55%	59	Marcel	95%
06	Andrew	90%	33	Edward	95%	60	Margaret	90%
07	Anne	20%	34	Elizabeth	95%	61	Martha	60%
08	Anthony	35%	35	Emil	05%	62	Mary	95%
09	Antoinette	10%	36	Eugenia	40%	63	Maurice	80%
10	Baptiste	30%	37	Felix	20%	64	Michael	60%
11	Barnaby	80%	38	Frances	90%	65	Paul	25%
12	Bartholomew	95%	39	Frank	95%	66	Peter	65%
13	Bernard	55%	40	Gabriel	80%	67	Philip	50%
14	Bertha	25%	41	Genevieve	05%	68	Raymond	95%
15	Camille (M)	80%	42	George	50%	69	Robert	80%
16	Catherine	10%	43	Gerard	75%	70	Stephen	85%
17	Cecilia	95%	44	Guy	20%	71	Theresa	35%
18	Charles	90%	45	Helen	50%	72	Thomas	20%
19	Christine	15%	46	Henrietta	40%	73	Victor	95%
20	Christopher	50%	47	Henry	80%	74	Vincent	70%
21	Claire	20%	48	Hugh	50%	75	Virginia	90%
22	Claude	30%	49	Jacqueline	95%	76	William	95%
23	Claudia	45%	50	James	80%	77	Yves	65%
24	Clement	80%	51	Jeanne	45%	78	Yvette	30%
25	Colette	70%	52	John	85%	79	Yvonne	05%
26	Daniel	45%	53	Joseph	80%			
27	Danielle	50%	54	Leon	40%			

**These are pilot names. See PART II: NAME DIRECTORY
for your associated pilot name.**

44

How *Guy* Relates To . . .

01	Agnes	35%	28	Denise	45%	55	Louis	80%
02	Albert	85%	29	Dennis	80%	56	Louise	95%
03	Alfred	55%	30	Dominic	60%	57	Lucien	95%
04	Alphonse	45%	31	Dominique	95%	58	Madeline	05%
05	Andrea	95%	32	Edmund	85%	59	Marcel	95%
06	Andrew	80%	33	Edward	30%	60	Margaret	50%
07	Anne	95%	34	Elizabeth	60%	61	Martha	80%
08	Anthony	45%	35	Emil	20%	62	Mary	95%
09	Antoinette	55%	36	Eugenia	20%	63	Maurice	45%
10	Baptiste	40%	37	Felix	85%	64	Michael	95%
11	Barnaby	95%	38	Frances	45%	65	Paul	95%
12	Bartholomew	40%	39	Frank	95%	66	Peter	80%
13	Bernard	90%	40	Gabriel	90%	67	Philip	30%
14	Bertha	70%	41	Genevieve	30%	68	Raymond	95%
15	Camille (M)	90%	42	George	60%	69	Robert	90%
16	Catherine	20%	43	Gerard	45%	70	Stephen	95%
17	Cecilia	95%	44	Guy	90%	71	Theresa	25%
18	Charles	45%	45	Helen	50%	72	Thomas	50%
19	Christine	50%	46	Henrietta	40%	73	Victor	15%
20	Christopher	95%	47	Henry	80%	74	Vincent	95%
21	Claire	30%	48	Hugh	10%	75	Virginia	40%
22	Claude	50%	49	Jacqueline	95%	76	William	95%
23	Claudia	40%	50	James	90%	77	Yves	95%
24	Clement	95%	51	Jeanne	30%	78	Yvette	10%
25	Colette	95%	52	John	95%	79	Yvonne	20%
26	Daniel	90%	53	Joseph	50%			
27	Danielle	95%	54	Leon	20%			

**These are pilot names. See PART II: NAME DIRECTORY
for your associated pilot name.**

45

How *Helen* Relates To . . .

01 Agnes	60%	28 Denise	05%	55 Louis	95%
02 Albert	95%	29 Dennis	40%	56 Louise	45%
03 Alfred	15%	30 Dominic	95%	57 Lucien	55%
04 Alphonse	55%	31 Dominique	30%	58 Madeline	95%
05 Andrea	85%	32 Edmund	70%	59 Marcel	95%
06 Andrew	95%	33 Edward	35%	60 Margaret	30%
07 Anne	30%	34 Elizabeth	80%	61 Martha	90%
08 Anthony	45%	35 Emil	15%	62 Mary	95%
09 Antoinette	20%	36 Eugenia	35%	63 Maurice	60%
10 Baptiste	50%	37 Felix	50%	64 Michael	95%
11 Barnaby	40%	38 Frances	55%	65 Paul	90%
12 Bartholomew	85%	39 Frank	95%	66 Peter	95%
13 Bernard	45%	40 Gabriel	95%	67 Philip	45%
14 Bertha	30%	41 Genevieve	05%	68 Raymond	95%
15 Camille (M)	95%	42 George	80%	69 Robert	95%
16 Catherine	45%	43 Gerard	45%	70 Stephen	95%
17 Cecilia	95%	44 Guy	40%	71 Theresa	20%
18 Charles	95%	45 Helen	60%	72 Thomas	95%
19 Christine	15%	46 Henrietta	40%	73 Victor	60%
20 Christopher	95%	47 Henry	95%	74 Vincent	25%
21 Claire	95%	48 Hugh	70%	75 Virginia	95%
22 Claude	70%	49 Jacqueline	95%	76 William	95%
23 Claudia	95%	50 James	95%	77 Yves	95%
24 Clement	40%	51 Jeanne	15%	78 Yvette	35%
25 Colette	95%	52 John	85%	79 Yvonne	15%
26 Daniel	50%	53 Joseph	90%		
27 Danielle	35%	54 Leon	45%		

These are pilot names. See PART II: NAME DIRECTORY for your associated pilot name.

46

How *Henrietta* Relates To . . .

01 Agnes	30%	28 Denise	40%	55 Louis	95%
02 Albert	70%	29 Dennis	15%	56 Louise	80%
03 Alfred	40%	30 Dominic	95%	57 Lucien	60%
04 Alphonse	20%	31 Dominique	30%	58 Madeline	10%
05 Andrea	95%	32 Edmund	95%	59 Marcel	95%
06 Andrew	80%	33 Edward	40%	60 Margaret	40%
07 Anne	95%	34 Elizabeth	50%	61 Martha	60%
08 Anthony	80%	35 Emil	30%	62 Mary	95%
09 Antoinette	60%	36 Eugenia	10%	63 Maurice	95%
10 Baptiste	30%	37 Felix	95%	64 Michael	95%
11 Barnaby	50%	38 Frances	40%	65 Paul	50%
12 Bartholomew	80%	39 Frank	85%	66 Peter	90%
13 Bernard	95%	40 Gabriel	95%	67 Philip	85%
14 Bertha	45%	41 Genevieve	20%	68 Raymond	35%
15 Camille (M)	80%	42 George	50%	69 Robert	70%
16 Catherine	95%	43 Gerard	95%	70 Stephen	90%
17 Cecilia	65%	44 Guy	20%	71 Theresa	45%
18 Charles	95%	45 Helen	95%	72 Thomas	95%
19 Christine	45%	46 Henrietta	20%	73 Victor	95%
20 Christopher	60%	47 Henry	80%	74 Vincent	50%
21 Claire	95%	48 Hugh	40%	75 Virginia	95%
22 Claude	55%	49 Jacqueline	80%	76 William	95%
23 Claudia	85%	50 James	95%	77 Yves	85%
24 Clement	95%	51 Jeanne	50%	78 Yvette	95%
25 Colette	95%	52 John	90%	79 Yvonne	45%
26 Daniel	50%	53 Joseph	65%		
27 Danielle	45%	54 Leon	30%		

These are pilot names. See **PART II: NAME DIRECTORY** for your associated pilot name.

| 47 |

How *Henry* Relates To . . .

01 Agnes	95%		28 Denise	25%		55 Louis	95%
02 Albert	85%		29 Dennis	95%		56 Louise	45%
03 Alfred	95%		30 Dominic	80%		57 Lucien	95%
04 Alphonse	90%		31 Dominique	95%		58 Madeline	40%
05 Andrea	95%		32 Edmund	95%		59 Marcel	95%
06 Andrew	95%		33 Edward	45%		60 Margaret	80%
07 Anne	90%		34 Elizabeth	55%		61 Martha	30%
08 Anthony	95%		35 Emil	95%		62 Mary	95%
09 Antoinette	60%		36 Eugenia	45%		63 Maurice	95%
10 Baptiste	95%		37 Felix	95%		64 Michael	45%
11 Barnaby	45%		38 Frances	40%		65 Paul	80%
12 Bartholomew	95%		39 Frank	90%		66 Peter	95%
13 Bernard	90%		40 Gabriel	95%		67 Philip	95%
14 Bertha	50%		41 Genevieve	10%		68 Raymond	75%
15 Camille (M)	95%		42 George	90%		69 Robert	90%
16 Catherine	60%		43 Gerard	50%		70 Stephen	85%
17 Cecilia	95%		44 Guy	80%		71 Theresa	35%
18 Charles	95%		45 Helen	45%		72 Thomas	95%
19 Christine	30%		46 Henrietta	30%		73 Victor	95%
20 Christopher	60%		47 Henry	85%		74 Vincent	95%
21 Claire	95%		48 Hugh	90%		75 Virginia	30%
22 Claude	80%		49 Jacqueline	95%		76 William	95%
23 Claudia	95%		50 James	95%		77 Yves	95%
24 Clement	95%		51 Jeanne	35%		78 Yvette	45%
25 Colette	60%		52 John	55%		79 Yvonne	95%
26 Daniel	50%		53 Joseph	95%			
27 Danielle	40%		54 Leon	95%			

These are pilot names. See **PART II: NAME DIRECTORY** for your associated pilot name.

48

How *Hugh* Relates To . . .

01 Agnes	50%	28 Denise	15%	55 Louis	45%
02 Albert	85%	29 Dennis	50%	56 Louise	95%
03 Alfred	90%	30 Dominic	95%	57 Lucien	80%
04 Alphonse	95%	31 Dominique	95%	58 Madeline	30%
05 Andrea	35%	32 Edmund	60%	59 Marcel	95%
06 Andrew	55%	33 Edward	45%	60 Margaret	30%
07 Anne	60%	34 Elizabeth	05%	61 Martha	10%
08 Anthony	40%	35 Emil	95%	62 Mary	90%
09 Antoinette	85%	36 Eugenia	25%	63 Maurice	95%
10 Baptiste	20%	37 Felix	95%	64 Michael	60%
11 Barnaby	90%	38 Frances	80%	65 Paul	20%
12 Bartholomew	50%	39 Frank	95%	66 Peter	70%
13 Bernard	95%	40 Gabriel	90%	67 Philip	50%
14 Bertha	15%	41 Genevieve	30%	68 Raymond	20%
15 Camille (M)	55%	42 George	50%	69 Robert	95%
16 Catherine	95%	43 Gerard	95%	70 Stephen	50%
17 Cecilia	95%	44 Guy	90%	71 Theresa	95%
18 Charles	10%	45 Helen	15%	72 Thomas	50%
19 Christine	40%	46 Henrietta	90%	73 Victor	95%
20 Christopher	95%	47 Henry	95%	74 Vincent	95%
21 Claire	50%	48 Hugh	95%	75 Virginia	50%
22 Claude	45%	49 Jacqueline	95%	76 William	95%
23 Claudia	95%	50 James	95%	77 Yves	95%
24 Clement	10%	51 Jeanne	95%	78 Yvette	60%
25 Colette	95%	52 John	20%	79 Yvonne	95%
26 Daniel	45%	53 Joseph	50%		
27 Danielle	95%	54 Leon	95%		

These are pilot names. See PART II: NAME DIRECTORY for your associated pilot name.

49

How *Jacqueline* Relates To . . .

01 Agnes	80%	28 Denise	95%	55 Louis	50%
02 Albert	50%	29 Dennis	50%	56 Louise	20%
03 Alfred	95%	30 Dominic	05%	57 Lucien	80%
04 Alphonse	10%	31 Dominique	95%	58 Madeline	50%
05 Andrea	50%	32 Edmund	80%	59 Marcel	95%
06 Andrew	95%	33 Edward	10%	60 Margaret	60%
07 Anne	95%	34 Elizabeth	85%	61 Martha	90%
08 Anthony	45%	35 Emil	50%	62 Mary	95%
09 Antoinette	25%	36 Eugenia	50%	63 Maurice	50%
10 Baptiste	80%	37 Felix	95%	64 Michael	30%
11 Barnaby	50%	38 Frances	95%	65 Paul	90%
12 Bartholomew	60%	39 Frank	10%	66 Peter	50%
13 Bernard	95%	40 Gabriel	95%	67 Philip	95%
14 Bertha	60%	41 Genevieve	10%	68 Raymond	45%
15 Camille (M)	45%	42 George	80%	69 Robert	50%
16 Catherine	55%	43 Gerard	60%	70 Stephen	95%
17 Cecilia	95%	44 Guy	45%	71 Theresa	95%
18 Charles	30%	45 Helen	80%	72 Thomas	80%
19 Christine	95%	46 Henrietta	40%	73 Victor	95%
20 Christopher	30%	47 Henry	95%	74 Vincent	10%
21 Claire	95%	48 Hugh	80%	75 Virginia	95%
22 Claude	20%	49 Jacqueline	10%	76 William	95%
23 Claudia	80%	50 James	05%	77 Yves	30%
24 Clement	50%	51 Jeanne	40%	78 Yvette	95%
25 Colette	95%	52 John	90%	79 Yvonne	25%
26 Daniel	25%	53 Joseph	95%		
27 Danielle	90%	54 Leon	45%		

**These are pilot names. See PART II: NAME DIRECTORY
for your associated pilot name.**

50

How *James* Relates To . . .

01 Agnes	70%	28 Denise	25%	55 Louis	85%
02 Albert	35%	29 Dennis	15%	56 Louise	70%
03 Alfred	45%	30 Dominic	60%	57 Lucien	45%
04 Alphonse	75%	31 Dominique	90%	58 Madeline	25%
05 Andrea	90%	32 Edmund	50%	59 Marcel	90%
06 Andrew	95%	33 Edward	30%	60 Margaret	80%
07 Anne	95%	34 Elizabeth	25%	61 Martha	90%
08 Anthony	70%	35 Emil	40%	62 Mary	95%
09 Antoinette	50%	36 Eugenia	45%	63 Maurice	20%
10 Baptiste	90%	37 Felix	10%	64 Michael	95%
11 Barnaby	50%	38 Frances	50%	65 Paul	40%
12 Bartholomew	45%	39 Frank	60%	66 Peter	80%
13 Bernard	20%	40 Gabriel	95%	67 Philip	95%
14 Bertha	55%	41 Genevieve	05%	68 Raymond	55%
15 Camille (M)	40%	42 George	20%	69 Robert	95%
16 Catherine	10%	43 Gerard	50%	70 Stephen	85%
17 Cecilia	65%	44 Guy	50%	71 Theresa	20%
18 Charles	80%	45 Helen	75%	72 Thomas	95%
19 Christine	25%	46 Henrietta	75%	73 Victor	30%
20 Christopher	85%	47 Henry	90%	74 Vincent	95%
21 Claire	60%	48 Hugh	85%	75 Virginia	75%
22 Claude	75%	49 Jacqueline	30%	76 William	40%
23 Claudia	60%	50 James	20%	77 Yves	20%
24 Clement	40%	51 Jeanne	50%	78 Yvette	90%
25 Colette	95%	52 John	40%	79 Yvonne	30%
26 Daniel	35%	53 Joseph	90%		
27 Danielle	45%	54 Leon	25%		

These are pilot names. See **PART II: NAME DIRECTORY** for your associated pilot name.

51

How *Jeanne* Relates To . . .

01	Agnes	30%	28	Denise	50%	55	Louis	90%
02	Albert	60%	29	Dennis	35%	56	Louise	60%
03	Alfred	90%	30	Dominic	95%	57	Lucien	45%
04	Alphonse	50%	31	Dominique	20%	58	Madeline	05%
05	Andrea	70%	32	Edmund	40%	59	Marcel	60%
06	Andrew	95%	33	Edward	95%	60	Margaret	10%
07	Anne	55%	34	Elizabeth	50%	61	Martha	55%
08	Anthony	20%	35	Emil	85%	62	Mary	95%
09	Antoinette	60%	36	Eugenia	30%	63	Maurice	30%
10	Baptiste	90%	37	Felix	60%	64	Michael	95%
11	Barnaby	90%	38	Frances	45%	65	Paul	30%
12	Bartholomew	60%	39	Frank	50%	66	Peter	60%
13	Bernard	30%	40	Gabriel	95%	67	Philip	50%
14	Bertha	50%	41	Genevieve	20%	68	Raymond	45%
15	Camille (M)	95%	42	George	50%	69	Robert	95%
16	Catherine	25%	43	Gerard	50%	70	Stephen	95%
17	Cecilia	05%	44	Guy	60%	71	Theresa	05%
18	Charles	75%	45	Helen	15%	72	Thomas	95%
19	Christine	45%	46	Henrietta	95%	73	Victor	30%
20	Christopher	80%	47	Henry	50%	74	Vincent	10%
21	Claire	50%	48	Hugh	65%	75	Virginia	95%
22	Claude	60%	49	Jacqueline	95%	76	William	95%
23	Claudia	95%	50	James	75%	77	Yves	95%
24	Clement	35%	51	Jeanne	45%	78	Yvette	80%
25	Colette	60%	52	John	50%	79	Yvonne	95%
26	Daniel	50%	53	Joseph	95%			
27	Danielle	90%	54	Leon	20%			

These are pilot names. See PART II: NAME DIRECTORY for your associated pilot name.

52

How *John* Relates To . . .

01 Agnes	85%	28 Denise	05%	55 Louis	95%
02 Albert	50%	29 Dennis	50%	56 Louise	20%
03 Alfred	80%	30 Dominic	85%	57 Lucien	85%
04 Alphonse	40%	31 Dominique	95%	58 Madeline	50%
05 Andrea	90%	32 Edmund	75%	59 Marcel	95%
06 Andrew	95%	33 Edward	45%	60 Margaret	60%
07 Anne	95%	34 Elizabeth	95%	61 Martha	95%
08 Anthony	45%	35 Emil	20%	62 Mary	95%
09 Antoinette	20%	36 Eugenia	50%	63 Maurice	90%
10 Baptiste	95%	37 Felix	70%	64 Michael	95%
11 Barnaby	40%	38 Frances	20%	65 Paul	95%
12 Bartholomew	75%	39 Frank	50%	66 Peter	70%
13 Bernard	25%	40 Gabriel	95%	67 Philip	40%
14 Bertha	50%	41 Genevieve	95%	68 Raymond	30%
15 Camille (M)	90%	42 George	60%	69 Robert	90%
16 Catherine	95%	43 Gerard	90%	70 Stephen	60%
17 Cecilia	90%	44 Guy	70%	71 Theresa	50%
18 Charles	95%	45 Helen	75%	72 Thomas	95%
19 Christine	30%	46 Henrietta	50%	73 Victor	80%
20 Christopher	80%	47 Henry	95%	74 Vincent	95%
21 Claire	95%	48 Hugh	95%	75 Virginia	50%
22 Claude	50%	49 Jacqueline	95%	76 William	95%
23 Claudia	75%	50 James	60%	77 Yves	95%
24 Clement	90%	51 Jeanne	80%	78 Yvette	30%
25 Colette	95%	52 John	70%	79 Yvonne	95%
26 Daniel	25%	53 Joseph	95%		
27 Danielle	10%	54 Leon	95%		

These are pilot names. See PART II: NAME DIRECTORY for your associated pilot name.

53

How *Joseph* Relates To . . .

01	Agnes	85%	28	Denise	50%	55	Louis	60%
02	Albert	95%	29	Dennis	20%	56	Louise	45%
03	Alfred	60%	30	Dominic	85%	57	Lucien	95%
04	Alphonse	50%	31	Dominique	95%	58	Madeline	45%
05	Andrea	95%	32	Edmund	80%	59	Marcel	80%
06	Andrew	95%	33	Edward	50%	60	Margaret	45%
07	Anne	80%	34	Elizabeth	95%	61	Martha	85%
08	Anthony	60%	35	Emil	60%	62	Mary	95%
09	Antoinette	30%	36	Eugenia	55%	63	Maurice	65%
10	Baptiste	95%	37	Felix	95%	64	Michael	95%
11	Barnaby	85%	38	Frances	55%	65	Paul	55%
12	Bartholomew	40%	39	Frank	90%	66	Peter	95%
13	Bernard	95%	40	Gabriel	95%	67	Philip	80%
14	Bertha	45%	41	Genevieve	10%	68	Raymond	50%
15	Camille (M)	95%	42	George	85%	69	Robert	95%
16	Catherine	45%	43	Gerard	95%	70	Stephen	95%
17	Cecilia	60%	44	Guy	95%	71	Theresa	45%
18	Charles	95%	45	Helen	85%	72	Thomas	95%
19	Christine	45%	46	Henrietta	30%	73	Victor	70%
20	Christopher	95%	47	Henry	95%	74	Vincent	55%
21	Claire	80%	48	Hugh	95%	75	Virginia	90%
22	Claude	85%	49	Jacqueline	95%	76	William	40%
23	Claudia	45%	50	James	95%	77	Yves	95%
24	Clement	60%	51	Jeanne	10%	78	Yvette	95%
25	Colette	90%	52	John	40%	79	Yvonne	60%
26	Daniel	45%	53	Joseph	95%			
27	Danielle	55%	54	Leon	95%			

**These are pilot names. See PART II: NAME DIRECTORY
for your associated pilot name.**

54

How *Leon* Relates To . . .

01 Agnes	90%	28 Denise	35%	55 Louis	40%
02 Albert	95%	29 Dennis	45%	56 Louise	35%
03 Alfred	80%	30 Dominic	95%	57 Lucien	90%
04 Alphonse	95%	31 Dominique	95%	58 Madeline	45%
05 Andrea	95%	32 Edmund	45%	59 Marcel	95%
06 Andrew	90%	33 Edward	95%	60 Margaret	90%
07 Anne	60%	34 Elizabeth	20%	61 Martha	60%
08 Anthony	95%	35 Emil	55%	62 Mary	95%
09 Antoinette	90%	36 Eugenia	90%	63 Maurice	90%
10 Baptiste	95%	37 Felix	95%	64 Michael	95%
11 Barnaby	95%	38 Frances	95%	65 Paul	95%
12 Bartholomew	50%	39 Frank	95%	66 Peter	95%
13 Bernard	35%	40 Gabriel	95%	67 Philip	95%
14 Bertha	65%	41 Genevieve	30%	68 Raymond	80%
15 Camille (M)	95%	42 George	90%	69 Robert	60%
16 Catherine	40%	43 Gerard	80%	70 Stephen	95%
17 Cecilia	95%	44 Guy	45%	71 Theresa	95%
18 Charles	60%	45 Helen	60%	72 Thomas	95%
19 Christine	50%	46 Henrietta	45%	73 Victor	30%
20 Christopher	95%	47 Henry	95%	74 Vincent	95%
21 Claire	90%	48 Hugh	95%	75 Virginia	80%
22 Claude	95%	49 Jacqueline	95%	76 William	55%
23 Claudia	45%	50 James	50%	77 Yves	95%
24 Clement	90%	51 Jeanne	95%	78 Yvette	90%
25 Colette	95%	52 John	95%	79 Yvonne	95%
26 Daniel	80%	53 Joseph	95%		
27 Danielle	55%	54 Leon	90%		

These are pilot names. See **PART II: NAME DIRECTORY**
for your associated pilot name.

COMPATIBILITY PERCENTAGES

55

How *Louis* Relates To . . .

01	Agnes	95%	28	Denise	50%	55	Louis	60%
02	Albert	95%	29	Dennis	95%	56	Louise	35%
03	Alfred	35%	30	Dominic	80%	57	Lucien	80%
04	Alphonse	50%	31	Dominique	95%	58	Madeline	30%
05	Andrea	95%	32	Edmund	95%	59	Marcel	85%
06	Andrew	95%	33	Edward	45%	60	Margaret	95%
07	Anne	95%	34	Elizabeth	95%	61	Martha	50%
08	Anthony	65%	35	Emil	95%	62	Mary	85%
09	Antoinette	40%	36	Eugenia	20%	63	Maurice	20%
10	Baptiste	80%	37	Felix	60%	64	Michael	95%
11	Barnaby	90%	38	Frances	80%	65	Paul	95%
12	Bartholomew	80%	39	Frank	50%	66	Peter	85%
13	Bernard	60%	40	Gabriel	90%	67	Philip	40%
14	Bertha	45%	41	Genevieve	05%	68	Raymond	95%
15	Camille (M)	55%	42	George	50%	69	Robert	95%
16	Catherine	95%	43	Gerard	70%	70	Stephen	40%
17	Cecilia	85%	44	Guy	85%	71	Theresa	50%
18	Charles	55%	45	Helen	85%	72	Thomas	95%
19	Christine	50%	46	Henrietta	50%	73	Victor	30%
20	Christopher	95%	47	Henry	95%	74	Vincent	95%
21	Claire	60%	48	Hugh	95%	75	Virginia	50%
22	Claude	95%	49	Jacqueline	95%	76	William	95%
23	Claudia	60%	50	James	60%	77	Yves	95%
24	Clement	20%	51	Jeanne	95%	78	Yvette	95%
25	Colette	55%	52	John	85%	79	Yvonne	10%
26	Daniel	95%	53	Joseph	45%			
27	Danielle	60%	54	Leon	50%			

These are pilot names. See PART II: NAME DIRECTORY for your associated pilot name.

56

How *Louise* Relates To . . .

01	Agnes	35%	28	Denise	85%	55	Louis	50%
02	Albert	60%	29	Dennis	95%	56	Louise	75%
03	Alfred	40%	30	Dominic	95%	57	Lucien	95%
04	Alphonse	05%	31	Dominique	95%	58	Madeline	05%
05	Andrea	45%	32	Edmund	20%	59	Marcel	50%
06	Andrew	95%	33	Edward	95%	60	Margaret	95%
07	Anne	85%	34	Elizabeth	85%	61	Martha	50%
08	Anthony	95%	35	Emil	60%	62	Mary	70%
09	Antoinette	40%	36	Eugenia	90%	63	Maurice	95%
10	Baptiste	95%	37	Felix	95%	64	Michael	90%
11	Barnaby	80%	38	Frances	50%	65	Paul	50%
12	Bartholomew	30%	39	Frank	10%	66	Peter	50%
13	Bernard	50%	40	Gabriel	95%	67	Philip	45%
14	Bertha	95%	41	Genevieve	95%	68	Raymond	95%
15	Camille (M)	55%	42	George	55%	69	Robert	50%
16	Catherine	95%	43	Gerard	95%	70	Stephen	45%
17	Cecilia	50%	44	Guy	50%	71	Theresa	95%
18	Charles	80%	45	Helen	85%	72	Thomas	95%
19	Christine	90%	46	Henrietta	45%	73	Victor	10%
20	Christopher	50%	47	Henry	95%	74	Vincent	50%
21	Claire	80%	48	Hugh	50%	75	Virginia	95%
22	Claude	40%	49	Jacqueline	95%	76	William	30%
23	Claudia	55%	50	James	45%	77	Yves	20%
24	Clement	25%	51	Jeanne	30%	78	Yvette	95%
25	Colette	95%	52	John	95%	79	Yvonne	95%
26	Daniel	20%	53	Joseph	95%			
27	Danielle	60%	54	Leon	30%			

These are pilot names. See PART II: NAME DIRECTORY for your associated pilot name.

COMPATIBILITY PERCENTAGES

57

How *Lucien* Relates To . . .

01	Agnes	90%	28	Denise	95%	55	Louis	80%
02	Albert	95%	29	Dennis	95%	56	Louise	20%
03	Alfred	20%	30	Dominic	95%	57	Lucien	85%
04	Alphonse	60%	31	Dominique	05%	58	Madeline	95%
05	Andrea	95%	32	Edmund	95%	59	Marcel	85%
06	Andrew	80%	33	Edward	20%	60	Margaret	50%
07	Anne	15%	34	Elizabeth	95%	61	Martha	50%
08	Anthony	50%	35	Emil	95%	62	Mary	90%
09	Antoinette	10%	36	Eugenia	45%	63	Maurice	95%
10	Baptiste	90%	37	Felix	95%	64	Michael	85%
11	Barnaby	50%	38	Frances	55%	65	Paul	95%
12	Bartholomew	95%	39	Frank	90%	66	Peter	30%
13	Bernard	65%	40	Gabriel	95%	67	Philip	50%
14	Bertha	45%	41	Genevieve	95%	68	Raymond	85%
15	Camille (M)	95%	42	George	50%	69	Robert	30%
16	Catherine	30%	43	Gerard	95%	70	Stephen	50%
17	Cecilia	90%	44	Guy	30%	71	Theresa	45%
18	Charles	50%	45	Helen	50%	72	Thomas	50%
19	Christine	25%	46	Henrietta	90%	73	Victor	40%
20	Christopher	95%	47	Henry	95%	74	Vincent	95%
21	Claire	60%	48	Hugh	95%	75	Virginia	90%
22	Claude	50%	49	Jacqueline	20%	76	William	95%
23	Claudia	95%	50	James	95%	77	Yves	50%
24	Clement	95%	51	Jeanne	30%	78	Yvette	95%
25	Colette	65%	52	John	95%	79	Yvonne	95%
26	Daniel	95%	53	Joseph	95%			
27	Danielle	20%	54	Leon	60%			

These are pilot names. See **PART II: NAME DIRECTORY** for your associated pilot name.

58

How *Madeline* Relates To . . .

01 Agnes	35%	28 Denise	20%	55 Louis	50%
02 Albert	60%	29 Dennis	40%	56 Louise	95%
03 Alfred	80%	30 Dominic	60%	57 Lucien	45%
04 Alphonse	20%	31 Dominique	95%	58 Madeline	25%
05 Andrea	95%	32 Edmund	35%	59 Marcel	40%
06 Andrew	90%	33 Edward	05%	60 Margaret	95%
07 Anne	95%	34 Elizabeth	95%	61 Martha	95%
08 Anthony	15%	35 Emil	45%	62 Mary	95%
09 Antoinette	45%	36 Eugenia	95%	63 Maurice	10%
10 Baptiste	05%	37 Felix	45%	64 Michael	90%
11 Barnaby	45%	38 Frances	45%	65 Paul	50%
12 Bartholomew	30%	39 Frank	50%	66 Peter	50%
13 Bernard	95%	40 Gabriel	95%	67 Philip	90%
14 Bertha	05%	41 Genevieve	20%	68 Raymond	80%
15 Camille (M)	40%	42 George	85%	69 Robert	95%
16 Catherine	80%	43 Gerard	50%	70 Stephen	90%
17 Cecilia	50%	44 Guy	50%	71 Theresa	95%
18 Charles	95%	45 Helen	95%	72 Thomas	30%
19 Christine	10%	46 Henrietta	50%	73 Victor	45%
20 Christopher	50%	47 Henry	85%	74 Vincent	05%
21 Claire	90%	48 Hugh	95%	75 Virginia	95%
22 Claude	95%	49 Jacqueline	95%	76 William	80%
23 Claudia	95%	50 James	95%	77 Yves	45%
24 Clement	40%	51 Jeanne	65%	78 Yvette	90%
25 Colette	60%	52 John	90%	79 Yvonne	95%
26 Daniel	85%	53 Joseph	60%		
27 Danielle	30%	54 Leon	20%		

**These are pilot names. See PART II: NAME DIRECTORY
for your associated pilot name.**

59

How *Marcel* Relates To . . .

01 Agnes	80%	28 Denise	15%	55 Louis	95%
02 Albert	90%	29 Dennis	40%	56 Louise	20%
03 Alfred	50%	30 Dominic	45%	57 Lucien	50%
04 Alphonse	95%	31 Dominique	95%	58 Madeline	30%
05 Andrea	60%	32 Edmund	60%	59 Marcel	75%
06 Andrew	95%	33 Edward	55%	60 Margaret	95%
07 Anne	95%	34 Elizabeth	30%	61 Martha	90%
08 Anthony	85%	35 Emil	95%	62 Mary	95%
09 Antoinette	80%	36 Eugenia	05%	63 Maurice	50%
10 Baptiste	95%	37 Felix	95%	64 Michael	95%
11 Barnaby	40%	38 Frances	50%	65 Paul	80%
12 Bartholomew	45%	39 Frank	45%	66 Peter	95%
13 Bernard	85%	40 Gabriel	95%	67 Philip	55%
14 Bertha	95%	41 Genevieve	20%	68 Raymond	85%
15 Camille (M)	20%	42 George	80%	69 Robert	95%
16 Catherine	80%	43 Gerard	40%	70 Stephen	35%
17 Cecilia	65%	44 Guy	20%	71 Theresa	95%
18 Charles	95%	45 Helen	95%	72 Thomas	95%
19 Christine	30%	46 Henrietta	30%	73 Victor	15%
20 Christopher	95%	47 Henry	95%	74 Vincent	05%
21 Claire	95%	48 Hugh	95%	75 Virginia	60%
22 Claude	30%	49 Jacqueline	10%	76 William	95%
23 Claudia	85%	50 James	95%	77 Yves	85%
24 Clement	95%	51 Jeanne	50%	78 Yvette	95%
25 Colette	95%	52 John	85%	79 Yvonne	30%
26 Daniel	60%	53 Joseph	95%		
27 Danielle	45%	54 Leon	30%		

These are pilot names. See **PART II: NAME DIRECTORY** for your associated pilot name.

60

How *Margaret* Relates To . . .

01 Agnes	50%		28 Denise	90%		55 Louis	95%
02 Albert	85%		29 Dennis	95%		56 Louise	80%
03 Alfred	95%		30 Dominic	30%		57 Lucien	60%
04 Alphonse	90%		31 Dominique	95%		58 Madeline	50%
05 Andrea	60%		32 Edmund	50%		59 Marcel	95%
06 Andrew	95%		33 Edward	95%		60 Margaret	70%
07 Anne	95%		34 Elizabeth	95%		61 Martha	60%
08 Anthony	50%		35 Emil	90%		62 Mary	85%
09 Antoinette	45%		36 Eugenia	30%		63 Maurice	50%
10 Baptiste	20%		37 Felix	90%		64 Michael	95%
11 Barnaby	50%		38 Frances	20%		65 Paul	65%
12 Bartholomew	95%		39 Frank	95%		66 Peter	95%
13 Bernard	80%		40 Gabriel	80%		67 Philip	85%
14 Bertha	50%		41 Genevieve	95%		68 Raymond	95%
15 Camille (M)	95%		42 George	40%		69 Robert	55%
16 Catherine	85%		43 Gerard	95%		70 Stephen	50%
17 Cecilia	95%		44 Guy	80%		71 Theresa	80%
18 Charles	80%		45 Helen	50%		72 Thomas	95%
19 Christine	40%		46 Henrietta	30%		73 Victor	90%
20 Christopher	95%		47 Henry	95%		74 Vincent	95%
21 Claire	95%		48 Hugh	95%		75 Virginia	50%
22 Claude	60%		49 Jacqueline	80%		76 William	45%
23 Claudia	95%		50 James	60%		77 Yves	95%
24 Clement	95%		51 Jeanne	95%		78 Yvette	95%
25 Colette	45%		52 John	95%		79 Yvonne	45%
26 Daniel	55%		53 Joseph	85%			
27 Danielle	40%		54 Leon	50%			

**These are pilot names. See PART II: NAME DIRECTORY
for your associated pilot name.**

61

How *Martha* Relates To . . .

01	Agnes	20%	28	Denise	45%	55	Louis	95%
02	Albert	90%	29	Dennis	95%	56	Louise	30%
03	Alfred	60%	30	Dominic	50%	57	Lucien	90%
04	Alphonse	95%	31	Dominique	95%	58	Madeline	45%
05	Andrea	95%	32	Edmund	95%	59	Marcel	70%
06	Andrew	65%	33	Edward	95%	60	Margaret	45%
07	Anne	50%	34	Elizabeth	45%	61	Martha	80%
08	Anthony	95%	35	Emil	90%	62	Mary	95%
09	Antoinette	20%	36	Eugenia	45%	63	Maurice	60%
10	Baptiste	90%	37	Felix	95%	64	Michael	90%
11	Barnaby	70%	38	Frances	30%	65	Paul	25%
12	Bartholomew	75%	39	Frank	90%	66	Peter	35%
13	Bernard	30%	40	Gabriel	85%	67	Philip	95%
14	Bertha	55%	41	Genevieve	05%	68	Raymond	95%
15	Camille (M)	95%	42	George	95%	69	Robert	65%
16	Catherine	40%	43	Gerard	40%	70	Stephen	55%
17	Cecilia	95%	44	Guy	60%	71	Theresa	15%
18	Charles	80%	45	Helen	40%	72	Thomas	50%
19	Christine	45%	46	Henrietta	40%	73	Victor	95%
20	Christopher	80%	47	Henry	95%	74	Vincent	05%
21	Claire	95%	48	Hugh	95%	75	Virginia	95%
22	Claude	85%	49	Jacqueline	20%	76	William	95%
23	Claudia	30%	50	James	80%	77	Yves	20%
24	Clement	40%	51	Jeanne	85%	78	Yvette	95%
25	Colette	95%	52	John	50%	79	Yvonne	95%
26	Daniel	35%	53	Joseph	95%			
27	Danielle	10%	54	Leon	50%			

These are pilot names. See PART II: NAME DIRECTORY for your associated pilot name.

62

How *Mary* Relates To . . .

01 Agnes	80%	28 Denise	45%	55 Louis	95%
02 Albert	95%	29 Dennis	80%	56 Louise	50%
03 Alfred	50%	30 Dominic	95%	57 Lucien	95%
04 Alphonse	90%	31 Dominique	85%	58 Madeline	95%
05 Andrea	80%	32 Edmund	30%	59 Marcel	90%
06 Andrew	95%	33 Edward	50%	60 Margaret	55%
07 Anne	95%	34 Elizabeth	90%	61 Martha	95%
08 Anthony	40%	35 Emil	40%	62 Mary	95%
09 Antoinette	50%	36 Eugenia	85%	63 Maurice	85%
10 Baptiste	95%	37 Felix	95%	64 Michael	95%
11 Barnaby	45%	38 Frances	95%	65 Paul	95%
12 Bartholomew	60%	39 Frank	95%	66 Peter	95%
13 Bernard	95%	40 Gabriel	95%	67 Philip	60%
14 Bertha	50%	41 Genevieve	90%	68 Raymond	30%
15 Camille (M)	80%	42 George	65%	69 Robert	95%
16 Catherine	90%	43 Gerard	50%	70 Stephen	95%
17 Cecilia	30%	44 Guy	95%	71 Theresa	50%
18 Charles	95%	45 Helen	85%	72 Thomas	95%
19 Christine	80%	46 Henrietta	35%	73 Victor	95%
20 Christopher	40%	47 Henry	60%	74 Vincent	20%
21 Claire	95%	48 Hugh	95%	75 Virginia	80%
22 Claude	95%	49 Jacqueline	55%	76 William	95%
23 Claudia	60%	50 James	95%	77 Yves	95%
24 Clement	90%	51 Jeanne	45%	78 Yvette	35%
25 Colette	95%	52 John	80%	79 Yvonne	40%
26 Daniel	45%	53 Joseph	95%		
27 Danielle	20%	54 Leon	30%		

**These are pilot names. See PART II: NAME DIRECTORY
for your associated pilot name.**

63

How *Maurice* Relates To . . .

01 Agnes	65%	28 Denise	50%	55 Louis	80%
02 Albert	95%	29 Dennis	45%	56 Louise	60%
03 Alfred	20%	30 Dominic	95%	57 Lucien	85%
04 Alphonse	95%	31 Dominique	05%	58 Madeline	20%
05 Andrea	85%	32 Edmund	95%	59 Marcel	95%
06 Andrew	30%	33 Edward	40%	60 Margaret	95%
07 Anne	50%	34 Elizabeth	50%	61 Martha	45%
08 Anthony	80%	35 Emil	90%	62 Mary	95%
09 Antoinette	15%	36 Eugenia	30%	63 Maurice	90%
10 Baptiste	95%	37 Felix	95%	64 Michael	90%
11 Barnaby	65%	38 Frances	80%	65 Paul	65%
12 Bartholomew	80%	39 Frank	95%	66 Peter	95%
13 Bernard	25%	40 Gabriel	95%	67 Philip	50%
14 Bertha	95%	41 Genevieve	95%	68 Raymond	40%
15 Camille (M)	90%	42 George	50%	69 Robert	85%
16 Catherine	50%	43 Gerard	30%	70 Stephen	95%
17 Cecilia	85%	44 Guy	50%	71 Theresa	20%
18 Charles	95%	45 Helen	35%	72 Thomas	95%
19 Christine	30%	46 Henrietta	60%	73 Victor	95%
20 Christopher	90%	47 Henry	85%	74 Vincent	05%
21 Claire	10%	48 Hugh	55%	75 Virginia	95%
22 Claude	95%	49 Jacqueline	95%	76 William	60%
23 Claudia	35%	50 James	95%	77 Yves	90%
24 Clement	65%	51 Jeanne	50%	78 Yvette	50%
25 Colette	90%	52 John	95%	79 Yvonne	15%
26 Daniel	45%	53 Joseph	95%		
27 Danielle	40%	54 Leon	30%		

These are pilot names. See **PART II: NAME DIRECTORY** for your associated pilot name.

64

How *Michael* Relates To . . .

01 Agnes	80%		28 Denise	70%		55 Louis	70%
02 Albert	95%		29 Dennis	95%		56 Louise	85%
03 Alfred	60%		30 Dominic	40%		57 Lucien	95%
04 Alphonse	80%		31 Dominique	80%		58 Madeline	30%
05 Andrea	90%		32 Edmund	95%		59 Marcel	80%
06 Andrew	95%		33 Edward	50%		60 Margaret	50%
07 Anne	95%		34 Elizabeth	65%		61 Martha	90%
08 Anthony	50%		35 Emil	90%		62 Mary	95%
09 Antoinette	30%		36 Eugenia	25%		63 Maurice	95%
10 Baptiste	95%		37 Felix	95%		64 Michael	15%
11 Barnaby	60%		38 Frances	80%		65 Paul	30%
12 Bartholomew	95%		39 Frank	65%		66 Peter	80%
13 Bernard	40%		40 Gabriel	95%		67 Philip	95%
14 Bertha	50%		41 Genevieve	55%		68 Raymond	40%
15 Camille (M)	75%		42 George	90%		69 Robert	85%
16 Catherine	95%		43 Gerard	40%		70 Stephen	95%
17 Cecilia	20%		44 Guy	70%		71 Theresa	50%
18 Charles	95%		45 Helen	75%		72 Thomas	95%
19 Christine	85%		46 Henrietta	80%		73 Victor	55%
20 Christopher	60%		47 Henry	95%		74 Vincent	15%
21 Claire	95%		48 Hugh	95%		75 Virginia	95%
22 Claude	35%		49 Jacqueline	50%		76 William	95%
23 Claudia	50%		50 James	95%		77 Yves	95%
24 Clement	90%		51 Jeanne	45%		78 Yvette	45%
25 Colette	95%		52 John	85%		79 Yvonne	50%
26 Daniel	45%		53 Joseph	70%			
27 Danielle	55%		54 Leon	50%			

**These are pilot names. See PART II: NAME DIRECTORY
for your associated pilot name.**

65

How *Paul* Relates To . . .

01 Agnes	65%		28 Denise	90%		55 Louis	95%
02 Albert	80%		29 Dennis	30%		56 Louise	40%
03 Alfred	90%		30 Dominic	60%		57 Lucien	95%
04 Alphonse	30%		31 Dominique	35%		58 Madeline	20%
05 Andrea	95%		32 Edmund	95%		59 Marcel	95%
06 Andrew	85%		33 Edward	50%		60 Margaret	90%
07 Anne	95%		34 Elizabeth	95%		61 Martha	45%
08 Anthony	45%		35 Emil	90%		62 Mary	95%
09 Antoinette	50%		36 Eugenia	60%		63 Maurice	80%
10 Baptiste	95%		37 Felix	50%		64 Michael	60%
11 Barnaby	40%		38 Frances	45%		65 Paul	20%
12 Bartholomew	50%		39 Frank	95%		66 Peter	95%
13 Bernard	95%		40 Gabriel	90%		67 Philip	85%
14 Bertha	50%		41 Genevieve	50%		68 Raymond	40%
15 Camille (M)	85%		42 George	40%		69 Robert	95%
16 Catherine	60%		43 Gerard	50%		70 Stephen	95%
17 Cecilia	95%		44 Guy	95%		71 Theresa	45%
18 Charles	95%		45 Helen	65%		72 Thomas	95%
19 Christine	20%		46 Henrietta	55%		73 Victor	95%
20 Christopher	90%		47 Henry	95%		74 Vincent	10%
21 Claire	95%		48 Hugh	30%		75 Virginia	95%
22 Claude	50%		49 Jacqueline	45%		76 William	95%
23 Claudia	95%		50 James	95%		77 Yves	95%
24 Clement	30%		51 Jeanne	45%		78 Yvette	30%
25 Colette	95%		52 John	95%		79 Yvonne	05%
26 Daniel	45%		53 Joseph	95%			
27 Danielle	10%		54 Leon	50%			

**These are pilot names. See PART II: NAME DIRECTORY
for your associated pilot name.**

66

How *Peter* Relates To . . .

01 Agnes	95%		28 Denise	45%		55 Louis	60%
02 Albert	30%		29 Dennis	10%		56 Louise	20%
03 Alfred	40%		30 Dominic	60%		57 Lucien	90%
04 Alphonse	05%		31 Dominique	95%		58 Madeline	40%
05 Andrea	95%		32 Edmund	65%		59 Marcel	95%
06 Andrew	95%		33 Edward	35%		60 Margaret	95%
07 Anne	95%		34 Elizabeth	90%		61 Martha	80%
08 Anthony	50%		35 Emil	30%		62 Mary	95%
09 Antoinette	55%		36 Eugenia	80%		63 Maurice	50%
10 Baptiste	90%		37 Felix	50%		64 Michael	95%
11 Barnaby	20%		38 Frances	65%		65 Paul	80%
12 Bartholomew	85%		39 Frank	35%		66 Peter	95%
13 Bernard	65%		40 Gabriel	95%		67 Philip	95%
14 Bertha	25%		41 Genevieve	10%		68 Raymond	70%
15 Camille (M)	40%		42 George	65%		69 Robert	95%
16 Catherine	90%		43 Gerard	45%		70 Stephen	95%
17 Cecilia	60%		44 Guy	45%		71 Theresa	20%
18 Charles	95%		45 Helen	70%		72 Thomas	95%
19 Christine	75%		46 Henrietta	95%		73 Victor	30%
20 Christopher	90%		47 Henry	95%		74 Vincent	05%
21 Claire	95%		48 Hugh	95%		75 Virginia	95%
22 Claude	50%		49 Jacqueline	95%		76 William	90%
23 Claudia	95%		50 James	95%		77 Yves	95%
24 Clement	95%		51 Jeanne	30%		78 Yvette	95%
25 Colette	95%		52 John	90%		79 Yvonne	25%
26 Daniel	40%		53 Joseph	95%			
27 Danielle	25%		54 Leon	30%			

**These are pilot names. See PART II: NAME DIRECTORY
for your associated pilot name.**

How *Philip* Relates To . . .

01 Agnes	95%	28 Denise	80%	55 Louis	95%
02 Albert	70%	29 Dennis	95%	56 Louise	80%
03 Alfred	50%	30 Dominic	95%	57 Lucien	50%
04 Alphonse	90%	31 Dominique	30%	58 Madeline	90%
05 Andrea	95%	32 Edmund	50%	59 Marcel	85%
06 Andrew	95%	33 Edward	10%	60 Margaret	45%
07 Anne	80%	34 Elizabeth	95%	61 Martha	95%
08 Anthony	95%	35 Emil	95%	62 Mary	80%
09 Antoinette	60%	36 Eugenia	55%	63 Maurice	95%
10 Baptiste	40%	37 Felix	95%	64 Michael	60%
11 Barnaby	95%	38 Frances	95%	65 Paul	80%
12 Bartholomew	85%	39 Frank	85%	66 Peter	90%
13 Bernard	55%	40 Gabriel	95%	67 Philip	80%
14 Bertha	95%	41 Genevieve	45%	68 Raymond	60%
15 Camille (M)	85%	42 George	90%	69 Robert	95%
16 Catherine	40%	43 Gerard	95%	70 Stephen	60%
17 Cecilia	85%	44 Guy	95%	71 Theresa	35%
18 Charles	95%	45 Helen	90%	72 Thomas	95%
19 Christine	35%	46 Henrietta	60%	73 Victor	60%
20 Christopher	85%	47 Henry	50%	74 Vincent	20%
21 Claire	50%	48 Hugh	90%	75 Virginia	50%
22 Claude	35%	49 Jacqueline	95%	76 William	65%
23 Claudia	90%	50 James	80%	77 Yves	95%
24 Clement	80%	51 Jeanne	50%	78 Yvette	70%
25 Colette	95%	52 John	95%	79 Yvonne	95%
26 Daniel	25%	53 Joseph	85%		
27 Danielle	10%	54 Leon	95%		

These are pilot names. See PART II: NAME DIRECTORY for your associated pilot name.

68

How *Raymond* Relates To . . .

01	Agnes	50%	28	Denise	55%	55	Louis	95%
02	Albert	95%	29	Dennis	85%	56	Louise	50%
03	Alfred	80%	30	Dominic	95%	57	Lucien	80%
04	Alphonse	95%	31	Dominique	25%	58	Madeline	20%
05	Andrea	60%	32	Edmund	95%	59	Marcel	95%
06	Andrew	85%	33	Edward	85%	60	Margaret	95%
07	Anne	95%	34	Elizabeth	95%	61	Martha	90%
08	Anthony	35%	35	Emil	50%	62	Mary	60%
09	Antoinette	90%	36	Eugenia	85%	63	Maurice	50%
10	Baptiste	95%	37	Felix	95%	64	Michael	85%
11	Barnaby	60%	38	Frances	80%	65	Paul	50%
12	Bartholomew	45%	39	Frank	90%	66	Peter	95%
13	Bernard	80%	40	Gabriel	90%	67	Philip	40%
14	Bertha	95%	41	Genevieve	30%	68	Raymond	60%
15	Camille (M)	90%	42	George	50%	69	Robert	95%
16	Catherine	95%	43	Gerard	85%	70	Stephen	40%
17	Cecilia	50%	44	Guy	95%	71	Theresa	15%
18	Charles	90%	45	Helen	85%	72	Thomas	95%
19	Christine	95%	46	Henrietta	50%	73	Victor	90%
20	Christopher	50%	47	Henry	90%	74	Vincent	95%
21	Claire	45%	48	Hugh	45%	75	Virginia	95%
22	Claude	95%	49	Jacqueline	55%	76	William	95%
23	Claudia	95%	50	James	95%	77	Yves	45%
24	Clement	95%	51	Jeanne	95%	78	Yvette	90%
25	Colette	40%	52	John	60%	79	Yvonne	95%
26	Daniel	85%	53	Joseph	90%			
27	Danielle	45%	54	Leon	95%			

**These are pilot names. See PART II: NAME DIRECTORY
for your associated pilot name.**

69

How *Robert* Relates To . . .

01	Agnes	95%	28	Denise	10%	55	Louis	90%
02	Albert	30%	29	Dennis	40%	56	Louise	85%
03	Alfred	85%	30	Dominic	95%	57	Lucien	50%
04	Alphonse	45%	31	Dominique	60%	58	Madeline	85%
05	Andrea	95%	32	Edmund	95%	59	Marcel	95%
06	Andrew	95%	33	Edward	95%	60	Margaret	45%
07	Anne	95%	34	Elizabeth	50%	61	Martha	50%
08	Anthony	40%	35	Emil	80%	62	Mary	95%
09	Antoinette	50%	36	Eugenia	95%	63	Maurice	35%
10	Baptiste	95%	37	Felix	95%	64	Michael	95%
11	Barnaby	60%	38	Frances	85%	65	Paul	70%
12	Bartholomew	95%	39	Frank	50%	66	Peter	95%
13	Bernard	35%	40	Gabriel	95%	67	Philip	90%
14	Bertha	70%	41	Genevieve	40%	68	Raymond	30%
15	Camille (M)	95%	42	George	80%	69	Robert	90%
16	Catherine	50%	43	Gerard	50%	70	Stephen	85%
17	Cecilia	90%	44	Guy	60%	71	Theresa	45%
18	Charles	95%	45	Helen	95%	72	Thomas	95%
19	Christine	50%	46	Henrietta	50%	73	Victor	50%
20	Christopher	95%	47	Henry	80%	74	Vincent	45%
21	Claire	95%	48	Hugh	30%	75	Virginia	95%
22	Claude	50%	49	Jacqueline	45%	76	William	95%
23	Claudia	80%	50	James	95%	77	Yves	50%
24	Clement	90%	51	Jeanne	60%	78	Yvette	95%
25	Colette	95%	52	John	90%	79	Yvonne	95%
26	Daniel	50%	53	Joseph	95%			
27	Danielle	30%	54	Leon	30%			

These are pilot names. See PART II: NAME DIRECTORY for your associated pilot name.

70

How *Stephen* Relates To . . .

01 Agnes	90%	28 Denise	95%	55 Louis	95%
02 Albert	95%	29 Dennis	30%	56 Louise	85%
03 Alfred	80%	30 Dominic	85%	57 Lucien	95%
04 Alphonse	75%	31 Dominique	45%	58 Madeline	40%
05 Andrea	85%	32 Edmund	95%	59 Marcel	95%
06 Andrew	95%	33 Edward	90%	60 Margaret	45%
07 Anne	95%	34 Elizabeth	60%	61 Martha	80%
08 Anthony	95%	35 Emil	80%	62 Mary	95%
09 Antoinette	60%	36 Eugenia	40%	63 Maurice	70%
10 Baptiste	90%	37 Felix	95%	64 Michael	90%
11 Barnaby	55%	38 Frances	55%	65 Paul	95%
12 Bartholomew	95%	39 Frank	90%	66 Peter	95%
13 Bernard	65%	40 Gabriel	95%	67 Philip	95%
14 Bertha	30%	41 Genevieve	50%	68 Raymond	80%
15 Camille (M)	50%	42 George	95%	69 Robert	95%
16 Catherine	40%	43 Gerard	70%	70 Stephen	60%
17 Cecilia	50%	44 Guy	80%	71 Theresa	30%
18 Charles	95%	45 Helen	85%	72 Thomas	50%
19 Christine	20%	46 Henrietta	85%	73 Victor	20%
20 Christopher	60%	47 Henry	95%	74 Vincent	80%
21 Claire	95%	48 Hugh	95%	75 Virginia	95%
22 Claude	80%	49 Jacqueline	80%	76 William	95%
23 Claudia	50%	50 James	95%	77 Yves	75%
24 Clement	95%	51 Jeanne	80%	78 Yvette	45%
25 Colette	75%	52 John	95%	79 Yvonne	50%
26 Daniel	55%	53 Joseph	95%		
27 Danielle	70%	54 Leon	90%		

**These are pilot names. See PART II: NAME DIRECTORY
for your associated pilot name.**

71

How *Theresa* Relates To . . .

01 Agnes	30%	28 Denise	40%	55 Louis	95%
02 Albert	80%	29 Dennis	50%	56 Louise	45%
03 Alfred	50%	30 Dominic	95%	57 Lucien	90%
04 Alphonse	10%	31 Dominique	20%	58 Madeline	50%
05 Andrea	95%	32 Edmund	95%	59 Marcel	35%
06 Andrew	85%	33 Edward	95%	60 Margaret	50%
07 Anne	95%	34 Elizabeth	90%	61 Martha	85%
08 Anthony	35%	35 Emil	30%	62 Mary	95%
09 Antoinette	60%	36 Eugenia	20%	63 Maurice	45%
10 Baptiste	45%	37 Felix	95%	64 Michael	95%
11 Barnaby	20%	38 Frances	05%	65 Paul	95%
12 Bartholomew	95%	39 Frank	10%	66 Peter	90%
13 Bernard	95%	40 Gabriel	60%	67 Philip	50%
14 Bertha	50%	41 Genevieve	05%	68 Raymond	95%
15 Camille (M)	45%	42 George	50%	69 Robert	30%
16 Catherine	95%	43 Gerard	20%	70 Stephen	95%
17 Cecilia	95%	44 Guy	90%	71 Theresa	30%
18 Charles	45%	45 Helen	10%	72 Thomas	95%
19 Christine	20%	46 Henrietta	45%	73 Victor	55%
20 Christopher	90%	47 Henry	95%	74 Vincent	05%
21 Claire	95%	48 Hugh	95%	75 Virginia	95%
22 Claude	30%	49 Jacqueline	60%	76 William	95%
23 Claudia	50%	50 James	50%	77 Yves	90%
24 Clement	95%	51 Jeanne	45%	78 Yvette	95%
25 Colette	95%	52 John	95%	79 Yvonne	95%
26 Daniel	30%	53 Joseph	95%		
27 Danielle	80%	54 Leon	50%		

These are pilot names. See **PART II: NAME DIRECTORY**
for your associated pilot name.

72

How *Thomas* Relates To . . .

01 Agnes	35%		28 Denise	95%		55 Louis	30%
02 Albert	85%		29 Dennis	40%		56 Louise	50%
03 Alfred	95%		30 Dominic	45%		57 Lucien	85%
04 Alphonse	80%		31 Dominique	10%		58 Madeline	30%
05 Andrea	95%		32 Edmund	50%		59 Marcel	65%
06 Andrew	75%		33 Edward	95%		60 Margaret	95%
07 Anne	50%		34 Elizabeth	95%		61 Martha	95%
08 Anthony	90%		35 Emil	85%		62 Mary	90%
09 Antoinette	40%		36 Eugenia	45%		63 Maurice	50%
10 Baptiste	60%		37 Felix	95%		64 Michael	95%
11 Barnaby	50%		38 Frances	90%		65 Paul	95%
12 Bartholomew	95%		39 Frank	50%		66 Peter	40%
13 Bernard	90%		40 Gabriel	95%		67 Philip	95%
14 Bertha	95%		41 Genevieve	05%		68 Raymond	95%
15 Camille (M)	95%		42 George	55%		69 Robert	55%
16 Catherine	90%		43 Gerard	80%		70 Stephen	65%
17 Cecilia	45%		44 Guy	20%		71 Theresa	80%
18 Charles	95%		45 Helen	45%		72 Thomas	70%
19 Christine	50%		46 Henrietta	85%		73 Victor	20%
20 Christopher	80%		47 Henry	95%		74 Vincent	95%
21 Claire	95%		48 Hugh	65%		75 Virginia	90%
22 Claude	50%		49 Jacqueline	50%		76 William	95%
23 Claudia	90%		50 James	95%		77 Yves	95%
24 Clement	45%		51 Jeanne	95%		78 Yvette	35%
25 Colette	80%		52 John	90%		79 Yvonne	50%
26 Daniel	25%		53 Joseph	85%			
27 Danielle	60%		54 Leon	50%			

These are pilot names. See PART II: NAME DIRECTORY for your associated pilot name.

73

How *Victor* Relates To . . .

01	Agnes	80%	28	Denise	20%	55	Louis	50%
02	Albert	90%	29	Dennis	60%	56	Louise	40%
03	Alfred	95%	30	Dominic	45%	57	Lucien	95%
04	Alphonse	95%	31	Dominique	95%	58	Madeline	30%
05	Andrea	90%	32	Edmund	80%	59	Marcel	95%
06	Andrew	95%	33	Edward	50%	60	Margaret	40%
07	Anne	95%	34	Elizabeth	95%	61	Martha	50%
08	Anthony	80%	35	Emil	55%	62	Mary	95%
09	Antoinette	10%	36	Eugenia	95%	63	Maurice	95%
10	Baptiste	95%	37	Felix	95%	64	Michael	95%
11	Barnaby	85%	38	Frances	45%	65	Paul	50%
12	Bartholomew	95%	39	Frank	20%	66	Peter	95%
13	Bernard	80%	40	Gabriel	85%	67	Philip	90%
14	Bertha	50%	41	Genevieve	55%	68	Raymond	55%
15	Camille (M)	95%	42	George	35%	69	Robert	95%
16	Catherine	90%	43	Gerard	50%	70	Stephen	95%
17	Cecilia	95%	44	Guy	90%	71	Theresa	20%
18	Charles	95%	45	Helen	50%	72	Thomas	80%
19	Christine	30%	46	Henrietta	30%	73	Victor	60%
20	Christopher	60%	47	Henry	95%	74	Vincent	95%
21	Claire	85%	48	Hugh	50%	75	Virginia	50%
22	Claude	45%	49	Jacqueline	95%	76	William	95%
23	Claudia	25%	50	James	95%	77	Yves	85%
24	Clement	95%	51	Jeanne	95%	78	Yvette	95%
25	Colette	35%	52	John	90%	79	Yvonne	95%
26	Daniel	40%	53	Joseph	95%			
27	Danielle	15%	54	Leon	50%			

These are pilot names. See PART II: NAME DIRECTORY for your associated pilot name.

74

How *Vincent* Relates To . . .

01 Agnes	90%	28 Denise	50%	55 Louis	70%
02 Albert	95%	29 Dennis	95%	56 Louise	45%
03 Alfred	30%	30 Dominic	60%	57 Lucien	95%
04 Alphonse	95%	31 Dominique	95%	58 Madeline	50%
05 Andrea	90%	32 Edmund	95%	59 Marcel	90%
06 Andrew	60%	33 Edward	95%	60 Margaret	95%
07 Anne	95%	34 Elizabeth	85%	61 Martha	40%
08 Anthony	45%	35 Emil	20%	62 Mary	60%
09 Antoinette	90%	36 Eugenia	50%	63 Maurice	80%
10 Baptiste	80%	37 Felix	85%	64 Michael	95%
11 Barnaby	90%	38 Frances	65%	65 Paul	50%
12 Bartholomew	40%	39 Frank	95%	66 Peter	95%
13 Bernard	95%	40 Gabriel	95%	67 Philip	85%
14 Bertha	60%	41 Genevieve	15%	68 Raymond	95%
15 Camille (M)	50%	42 George	50%	69 Robert	60%
16 Catherine	10%	43 Gerard	30%	70 Stephen	95%
17 Cecilia	50%	44 Guy	80%	71 Theresa	50%
18 Charles	95%	45 Helen	50%	72 Thomas	95%
19 Christine	45%	46 Henrietta	45%	73 Victor	95%
20 Christopher	95%	47 Henry	90%	74 Vincent	25%
21 Claire	30%	48 Hugh	95%	75 Virginia	65%
22 Claude	50%	49 Jacqueline	90%	76 William	95%
23 Claudia	95%	50 James	95%	77 Yves	95%
24 Clement	95%	51 Jeanne	10%	78 Yvette	10%
25 Colette	65%	52 John	50%	79 Yvonne	95%
26 Daniel	95%	53 Joseph	95%		
27 Danielle	20%	54 Leon	90%		

**These are pilot names. See PART II: NAME DIRECTORY
for your associated pilot name.**

75

How *Virginia* Relates To . . .

01 Agnes	55%		28 Denise	70%		55 Louis	45%
02 Albert	30%		29 Dennis	50%		56 Louise	60%
03 Alfred	40%		30 Dominic	85%		57 Lucien	40%
04 Alphonse	80%		31 Dominique	30%		58 Madeline	50%
05 Andrea	95%		32 Edmund	50%		59 Marcel	80%
06 Andrew	90%		33 Edward	05%		60 Margaret	60%
07 Anne	25%		34 Elizabeth	95%		61 Martha	20%
08 Anthony	45%		35 Emil	45%		62 Mary	90%
09 Antoinette	25%		36 Eugenia	20%		63 Maurice	60%
10 Baptiste	30%		37 Felix	60%		64 Michael	35%
11 Barnaby	90%		38 Frances	40%		65 Paul	85%
12 Bartholomew	45%		39 Frank	35%		66 Peter	20%
13 Bernard	30%		40 Gabriel	70%		67 Philip	30%
14 Bertha	95%		41 Genevieve	15%		68 Raymond	50%
15 Camille (M)	20%		42 George	55%		69 Robert	65%
16 Catherine	85%		43 Gerard	20%		70 Stephen	90%
17 Cecilia	60%		44 Guy	50%		71 Theresa	25%
18 Charles	40%		45 Helen	30%		72 Thomas	90%
19 Christine	95%		46 Henrietta	95%		73 Victor	25%
20 Christopher	15%		47 Henry	85%		74 Vincent	45%
21 Claire	95%		48 Hugh	30%		75 Virginia	85%
22 Claude	55%		49 Jacqueline	95%		76 William	70%
23 Claudia	45%		50 James	40%		77 Yves	20%
24 Clement	45%		51 Jeanne	50%		78 Yvette	95%
25 Colette	95%		52 John	95%		79 Yvonne	10%
26 Daniel	65%		53 Joseph	60%			
27 Danielle	45%		54 Leon	80%			

These are pilot names. See PART II: NAME DIRECTORY for your associated pilot name.

76

How *William* Relates To . . .

01	Agnes	95%	28	Denise	95%	55	Louis	95%
02	Albert	80%	29	Dennis	30%	56	Louise	40%
03	Alfred	95%	30	Dominic	50%	57	Lucien	95%
04	Alphonse	50%	31	Dominique	95%	58	Madeline	60%
05	Andrea	95%	32	Edmund	80%	59	Marcel	95%
06	Andrew	80%	33	Edward	95%	60	Margaret	30%
07	Anne	80%	34	Elizabeth	85%	61	Martha	95%
08	Anthony	95%	35	Emil	25%	62	Mary	90%
09	Antoinette	40%	36	Eugenia	50%	63	Maurice	95%
10	Baptiste	95%	37	Felix	90%	64	Michael	95%
11	Barnaby	60%	38	Frances	95%	65	Paul	30%
12	Bartholomew	50%	39	Frank	50%	66	Peter	95%
13	Bernard	95%	40	Gabriel	95%	67	Philip	50%
14	Bertha	55%	41	Genevieve	95%	68	Raymond	95%
15	Camille (M)	95%	42	George	50%	69	Robert	30%
16	Catherine	10%	43	Gerard	25%	70	Stephen	95%
17	Cecilia	85%	44	Guy	95%	71	Theresa	65%
18	Charles	95%	45	Helen	40%	72	Thomas	95%
19	Christine	30%	46	Henrietta	90%	73	Victor	30%
20	Christopher	85%	47	Henry	95%	74	Vincent	50%
21	Claire	95%	48	Hugh	45%	75	Virginia	95%
22	Claude	25%	49	Jacqueline	95%	76	William	70%
23	Claudia	85%	50	James	90%	77	Yves	95%
24	Clement	95%	51	Jeanne	40%	78	Yvette	20%
25	Colette	90%	52	John	70%	79	Yvonne	05%
26	Daniel	70%	53	Joseph	95%			
27	Danielle	85%	54	Leon	85%			

These are pilot names. See PART II: NAME DIRECTORY for your associated pilot name.

How **Yves** Relates To . . .

01	Agnes	95%	28	Denise	35%	55	Louis	55%
02	Albert	60%	29	Dennis	85%	56	Louise	90%
03	Alfred	50%	30	Dominic	95%	57	Lucien	75%
04	Alphonse	90%	31	Dominique	95%	58	Madeline	45%
05	Andrea	50%	32	Edmund	10%	59	Marcel	95%
06	Andrew	95%	33	Edward	85%	60	Margaret	90%
07	Anne	35%	34	Elizabeth	45%	61	Martha	50%
08	Anthony	85%	35	Emil	45%	62	Mary	95%
09	Antoinette	45%	36	Eugenia	90%	63	Maurice	35%
10	Baptiste	95%	37	Felix	35%	64	Michael	80%
11	Barnaby	95%	38	Frances	95%	65	Paul	95%
12	Bartholomew	50%	39	Frank	95%	66	Peter	45%
13	Bernard	30%	40	Gabriel	95%	67	Philip	95%
14	Bertha	90%	41	Genevieve	15%	68	Raymond	95%
15	Camille (M)	50%	42	George	80%	69	Robert	95%
16	Catherine	40%	43	Gerard	45%	70	Stephen	95%
17	Cecilia	55%	44	Guy	60%	71	Theresa	45%
18	Charles	80%	45	Helen	10%	72	Thomas	90%
19	Christine	45%	46	Henrietta	20%	73	Victor	80%
20	Christopher	80%	47	Henry	50%	74	Vincent	45%
21	Claire	95%	48	Hugh	70%	75	Virginia	85%
22	Claude	95%	49	Jacqueline	95%	76	William	95%
23	Claudia	60%	50	James	90%	77	Yves	95%
24	Clement	50%	51	Jeanne	95%	78	Yvette	95%
25	Colette	30%	52	John	95%	79	Yvonne	95%
26	Daniel	95%	53	Joseph	95%			
27	Danielle	40%	54	Leon	80%			

These are pilot names. See **PART II: NAME DIRECTORY** for your associated pilot name.

78

How *Yvette* Relates To . . .

01	Agnes	95%	28	Denise	40%	55	Louis	45%
02	Albert	20%	29	Dennis	45%	56	Louise	95%
03	Alfred	50%	30	Dominic	40%	57	Lucien	50%
04	Alphonse	05%	31	Dominique	95%	58	Madeline	45%
05	Andrea	95%	32	Edmund	30%	59	Marcel	95%
06	Andrew	90%	33	Edward	05%	60	Margaret	40%
07	Anne	50%	34	Elizabeth	95%	61	Martha	45%
08	Anthony	20%	35	Emil	95%	62	Mary	95%
09	Antoinette	85%	36	Eugenia	45%	63	Maurice	60%
10	Baptiste	95%	37	Felix	95%	64	Michael	40%
11	Barnaby	30%	38	Frances	50%	65	Paul	50%
12	Bartholomew	95%	39	Frank	45%	66	Peter	95%
13	Bernard	15%	40	Gabriel	95%	67	Philip	40%
14	Bertha	50%	41	Genevieve	10%	68	Raymond	95%
15	Camille (M)	45%	42	George	65%	69	Robert	95%
16	Catherine	95%	43	Gerard	55%	70	Stephen	85%
17	Cecilia	90%	44	Guy	95%	71	Theresa	45%
18	Charles	65%	45	Helen	40%	72	Thomas	95%
19	Christine	45%	46	Henrietta	50%	73	Victor	30%
20	Christopher	90%	47	Henry	90%	74	Vincent	05%
21	Claire	95%	48	Hugh	95%	75	Virginia	70%
22	Claude	95%	49	Jacqueline	95%	76	William	95%
23	Claudia	40%	50	James	95%	77	Yves	95%
24	Clement	50%	51	Jeanne	90%	78	Yvette	40%
25	Colette	95%	52	John	45%	79	Yvonne	95%
26	Daniel	40%	53	Joseph	95%			
27	Danielle	10%	54	Leon	95%			

These are pilot names. See PART II: NAME DIRECTORY for your associated pilot name.

COMPATIBILITY PERCENTAGES

79

How *Yvonne* Relates To . . .

01 Agnes	10%	28 Denise	65%	55 Louis	50%
02 Albert	60%	29 Dennis	30%	56 Louise	70%
03 Alfred	90%	30 Dominic	20%	57 Lucien	30%
04 Alphonse	20%	31 Dominique	20%	58 Madeline	50%
05 Andrea	60%	32 Edmund	50%	59 Marcel	95%
06 Andrew	95%	33 Edward	05%	60 Margaret	40%
07 Anne	95%	34 Elizabeth	25%	61 Martha	50%
08 Anthony	30%	35 Emil	50%	62 Mary	80%
09 Antoinette	40%	36 Eugenia	25%	63 Maurice	95%
10 Baptiste	50%	37 Felix	50%	64 Michael	60%
11 Barnaby	45%	38 Frances	55%	65 Paul	50%
12 Bartholomew	95%	39 Frank	70%	66 Peter	95%
13 Bernard	80%	40 Gabriel	95%	67 Philip	90%
14 Bertha	15%	41 Genevieve	40%	68 Raymond	20%
15 Camille (M)	90%	42 George	50%	69 Robert	95%
16 Catherine	10%	43 Gerard	45%	70 Stephen	40%
17 Cecilia	20%	44 Guy	45%	71 Theresa	20%
18 Charles	50%	45 Helen	50%	72 Thomas	50%
19 Christine	60%	46 Henrietta	60%	73 Victor	50%
20 Christopher	95%	47 Henry	80%	74 Vincent	05%
21 Claire	20%	48 Hugh	30%	75 Virginia	95%
22 Claude	50%	49 Jacqueline	50%	76 William	80%
23 Claudia	55%	50 James	90%	77 Yves	45%
24 Clement	85%	51 Jeanne	40%	78 Yvette	95%
25 Colette	50%	52 John	95%	79 Yvonne	05%
26 Daniel	60%	53 Joseph	60%		
27 Danielle	90%	54 Leon	45%		

These are pilot names. See **PART II: NAME DIRECTORY**
for your associated pilot name.

149